MW00561459

NEW YORK GREEN

NEW YORK GREEN

Discovering the City's Most Treasured Parks and Gardens

Written & photographed by

Ngoc Minh Ngo

ARTISAN | NEW YORK

Copyright © 2023 by Ngoc Minh Ngo

All rights reserved. No portion of this book may
be reproduced—mechanically, electronically, or by
any other means, including photocopying—without
written permission of the publisher.

Library of Congress Cataloging-in-Publication Data

Names: Ngo, Ngoc Minh, author.
Title: New York green / Ngoc Minh Ngo.
    Description: New York : Artisan, an imprint of
    Workman Publishing Co., Inc., 2023. | Includes
    index. | Summary: "Celebrated photographer
    Ngoc Minh Ngo takes readers on a tour of the
    most exceptional gardens and parks across New
    York City's five boroughs in this lushly illustrated
    book"—Provided by publisher.
Identifiers: LCCN 2022055149 | ISBN 9781648290732
    (hardcover) | ISBN 9781648293122 (ebook)
Subjects: LCSH: Parks—New York (State)—New York—
    Guidebooks. | Gardens—New York (State)—New
    York--Guidebooks. | New York (N.Y.)—Guidebooks.
Classification: LCC F128.65.A1 N46 2023 | DDC
    363.6/8097471—dc23/eng/20221115
LC record available at https://lccn.loc.gov/2022055149

Design by Vanessa Holden

Artisan books are available at special discounts
when purchased in bulk for premiums and sales
promotions as well as for fundraising or educational
use. Special editions or book excerpts can also be
created to specification. For details, please contact
specialmarkets@hbgusa.com.

Published by Artisan,
an imprint of Workman Publishing Co., Inc.,
a subsidiary of Hachette Book Group, Inc.
1290 Avenue of the Americas
New York, NY 10104
artisanbooks.com

Artisan is a registered trademark
of Workman Publishing Co., Inc.,
a subsidiary of Hachette Book Group, Inc.

Printed in China on responsibly sourced paper

First printing, April 2023

10 9 8 7 6 5 4 3 2 1

To all New Yorkers—past, present, future

Urban Pastoral

New York City's Green Spaces

The neurologist and author Oliver Sacks once wrote, "Biophilia, the love of nature and living things, is an essential part of the human condition." For Sacks, who lived and worked in New York for half a century, the city was made bearable "only by its gardens." For New Yorkers enduring the recent pandemic, the healing powers of gardens have been an incomparable solace. Walt Whitman's "city of spires and masts" is also grounded in a tapestry of green spaces that reflects the dynamic evolution of this fabled place in recent history.

In 1609, when Henry Hudson came upon the island of what was then called Mannahatta ("Island of Many Hills") by the Lenape, he found an ecological nirvana, teeming with natural wonders. Majestic American chestnuts ruled the forests with their towering heights, bearing prolific nuts that kept the white-tailed deer and passenger pigeons well fed in fall. Venerable giants—tulip trees, oaks, hickories, maples, sweet gum, and beech—filled the dense canopies that reached for the sky. In early spring, the dappled shade of the understory erupted with the blooms of flowering dogwoods, eastern redbuds, and mountain laurels. Ferns, orchids, red columbines, and white starflowers tangled at their feet. Hummingbirds fed on Turk's-cap lilies and cardinal flowers on the edge of woodlands. Wild roses, milkweeds, harlequin blue flags, and asters painted bright swaths of color in sunny meadows, delighting busy pollinators from spring to late autumn. Black bears feasted in highbush blueberry bogs. In coniferous bogs, Hessel's hairstreak butterflies—barely larger than an inch,

with emerald-green-tailed wings—flew high at the tip of Atlantic white cedars, mating and leaving their caterpillar offspring to feed on the cedar foliage. The grasslands in the flat plains, home of heath hens, also provided the breeding ground for bobolinks that made their nests on wet soil at the base of meadow rues. Millions of birds flocked to Mannahatta on their migratory paths, banqueting on the abundance of seeds, berries, and foliage on the island. As rendered by the landscape ecologist Eric W. Sanderson in his book *Mannahatta*, the land that lies beneath New York City was once an unimaginably rich ecosystem, having evolved through thousands of life cycles, enlivened by generations of interconnected flora and fauna.

The green paradise found by Hudson had all but vanished by the end of the nineteenth century. The island's forests had been cut down, its hills flattened, its streams and ponds emptied to make way for a bustling metropolis built on a rigid grid. The city's "swarming and multitudinous" population—in Walt Whitman's description—crowded into squalid slums with unhealthy air and no access to nature. New York was in dire need of open green spaces. "What are called parks in New-York are not even apologies for the thing; they are only squares or paddocks," decried the nurseryman turned writer Andrew Jackson Downing in 1850. Other civic-minded New Yorkers rallied to Downing's cause, the creation of a large public park, on the scale of those in European cities, for the benefit of all classes of society. Its construction, however, would end up forcing the displacement of Seneca Village, the largest community of Black property owners in pre–Civil War New York. Central Park opened to the public in 1858 with a design by Calvert Vaux and Frederick Law Olmsted, who declared the common person "the true owner of the park." Sweeping lawns, luxuriant woodlands, meandering streams, and limpid lakes offered all New Yorkers a pastoral escape. Vaux and Olmsted went on to create Prospect Park in Brooklyn, realizing their ideal vision of a city park, the aesthetic of the English landscape garden wedded to the American democratic creed. In 1888, the city quintupled its green space overnight with nearly four thousand acres above the Harlem River dedicated to six large parks—including Crotona, Van Cortlandt, and Pelham Bay Parks— and parkways.

As New York City's fortunes rose and fell in the following century, so did the state of its natural environments. In the 1970s, the city teetered on bankruptcy. Parks became neglected, abandoned, and mostly forgotten. Facing a crumbling city, ordinary New Yorkers stepped up to reclaim it with nature. Sixty-four-year-old Hattie Carthan sought to improve the quality of life on the barren streets of her Bedford-Stuyvesant neighborhood by planting trees. Rallying her neighbors and gaining the support of Mayor John Lindsay, she planted fifteen hundred gingko, sycamore, and honey locust trees on sidewalks within a few years. In the East Village, a group of young people led by an artist named Liz Christy rescued derelict spaces by planting flower boxes and community gardens. They called themselves the Green Guerillas, the twin evocation of nature and warfare summing

up some fundamental yet contradictory characteristics of New Yorkers, and perhaps even the city itself—tough, tenacious, yet tender. Uptown, concerned citizens formed the Central Park Conservancy to help salvage and maintain Vaux and Olmsted's masterpiece in partnership with the city's Parks Department. In the 1990s, Bette Midler's New York Restoration Project, founded by the entertainer to restore run-down parks, saved 114 community gardens from being sold off to developers.

In the following decade, faced with the challenges of climate change, New York became a greener city. On median strips, traffic circles, and street triangles, concrete was torn up to make miniature flower gardens. A million trees were planted in ten years, reinforcing the urban forest. In Long Island City, hulking gantries, emblems of the industry that dominated the waterfront for decades, became the symbols and namesake of a new park, a pleasure ground along the once-bleak shoreline. In the Meatpacking District near the West Side Highway, a disused railroad that had sat abandoned for years was reinvented as a public park. Woodlands shaded by slender birch trees and grasslands woven with prairie flowers sprang up between the railroad tracks, edged against the ziggurat of rooftops that define our skyline. Embracing both the urban and the pastoral, celebrating both the past and the future, Gantry Plaza State Park and the High Line celebrate and incorporate the city's industrial archaeology into our public parks.

Whereas Olmsted saw parks as an escape from the city, the landscape architect Michael

Van Valkenburgh sees them "as an escape in the city, and therefore an essential part of what a city is." The East River waterfront in Brooklyn, once a thriving harbor but barren and decrepit since the end of cargo ship operations in 1983, was reimagined by Van Valkenburgh as a sprawling eighty-five-acre park rooted in the concept of a "postindustrial nature." Materials that existed on the site from its former life were recycled and reinvented as park benches and cladding for new structures. Salt marshes and meadows were re-created to bring back the diverse ecologies that once existed on the shoreline. The reinvention of these waterfronts, notably with Brooklyn Bridge Park, Hudson River Park, and Hunter's Point South Park, has not only given residents and visitors magnificent and inventive parks but also highlights the city's vulnerabilities in the age of climate change. In twenty-first-century parks, nature is no longer just the backdrop for human recreation; instead, it claims a vital place in the urban environment. Plants are no longer seen as mere decoration but as part of an ecosystem that supports all life on the planet.

Vaux and Olmsted made Central Park for the people, but both humans and wildlife now find refuge in New York's green spaces. A mile of shoreline on Rockaway Beach is reserved during breeding season for piping plovers looking for a place to start a family. Bald eagles, once habitués of the Hudson River's estuary, have returned to Inwood Hill Park since 2001. The Naval Cemetery Landscape is as much a monarch butterfly way station as it is a memorial meadow, an urban retreat for both local residents and migrating birds and butterflies.

Today, green spaces take up nearly 15 percent of the city's 305 square miles. From tiny city lots to acres of old-growth forests, each has its own history, attractions, and interest. The twenty-first-century iteration of Mannahatta has a wealth of green spaces as diverse as its citizens—pristine coastlines and vibrant waterfront parks, resplendent botanical gardens and quirky community gardens, lush esplanades and inventive vest-pocket parks, wildflower meadows and formal flower gardens. They are places where New Yorkers gather, pause, play, chill, learn, and discover, offering not only Olmsted's "enlarged sense of freedom" but also an amplified sense of wonder and a deeper understanding of our place in the environment. The Mannahatta that the Lenape inhabited for four hundred generations has disappeared forever, its biodiversity replaced by cultural diversity. Nonetheless, its spirit lingers in the three million trees—both native and introduced species—that make up the city's urban forest, in the more than two hundred species of migrant birds and wildlife that have found their way back to the island as well as new arrivals, and in the hearts of over eight million New Yorkers. The city's green spaces, as multitudinous as its population, celebrate the uncommon beauty of this urban pastoral, much like a Walt Whitman poem.

New York Botanical Garden, page 19

Top Places for . . .

Kayaking

Nature Trails

Picnics

Public Art

Sunset Views

Hunter's Point South Park, page 239

Prospect Park, page 165

The Bronx

Pelham Bay Park

A wildlife haven and a man-made beach in New York City's biggest park

In 1876, Frederick Law Olmsted, hired to survey the Bronx, proposed a greenbelt of parkways and parks across the borough more befitting of the natural geography than the grid system in Manhattan. More than a decade later and after much debate, land was purchased to fulfill this vision, giving the borough six new parks. Among them was Pelham Bay Park, which combined twenty-eight private estates for 2,772 acres of parkland—making it the city's biggest park, at three times the size of Central Park.

This behemoth boasts two golf courses, a football field, four playgrounds, and numerous ball courts, among other amenities. But the park's natural attributes are its greatest appeal. Dominated by hundreds of acres of forest and woodland, miles of shoreline hugging Long Island Sound, vast flowering meadows, and bodies of water large and small—from vernal ponds to a big lagoon—Pelham Bay Park contains the wild beauty of the city's native ecology as well as the many human stories imprinted on this expanse of the city.

For those interested in reading the history embedded in its landscape, Hunter Island (pictured on the following pages) is a fascinating destination. A peninsula since the 1930s, the island was originally called Laaphawachking ("place of stringing beads") by the Siwanoys who lived in this area (it was renamed after John Hunter, who built a mansion on the island in the nineteenth century). The Kazimiroff Nature Trail winds through a forest of mature oak and hickory trees, native wildflowers, glacial rock formations, wetlands, and vestiges of Hunter's estate, each revealing a layer of the site's history. A thick stand of white pines is home to the island's great horned owls. The rocky shore, with its fertile salt marshes and graceful waterbirds, is a picturesque reminder of what parks advocate John Mullaly called "a margin that satisfies the imagination of the poet and the taste of the painter."

Pelham Bay Park's rugged beauty owes much to glacial erratics, boulders deposited some twenty thousand years ago by the flow of the Wisconsinan glacier. Today these rocks from the Ice Age are testaments to the park's rich geology and history. Split Rock, a twenty-five-foot-long boulder riven in half by glacial flow millennia ago, is both a geological wonder and a reification of the bloody history of an onslaught that killed the seventeenth-century religious rebel Anne Hutchinson and her family. In 2015, a trove of artifacts dating back to 200 CE was discovered in a southeastern section of the park, indicating the presence of Indigenous people in the area centuries before the arrival of European settlers.

Despite the park's natural beauty, its most popular feature is the man-made Orchard Beach. Affectionally known as the "Bronx Riviera," the mile-long crescent beach opened in 1936 with much fanfare—ten thousand New Yorkers in attendance and a lot of fireworks. In summer, thousands flock here to cool off, but in late autumn, it's a tranquil spot for a restorative walk on the sand and a resting locale for harbor seals.

A place of both natural beauty and artifice, a palimpsest of human history and a wildlife haven, Pelham Bay Park has something for everyone. For a certain moth subspecies, *Amphipoea erepta*, which has made its only home on Earth in a meadow here, the park is unique in all the world.

established 1888 **total acreage** 2,772 **entrance** Middletown Road and Stadium Avenue
public transit Pelham Bay Park ❻ **website** pelhambaypark.org

New York Botanical Garden

A wonderland for plants from around the world

Plants are a source of life. They feed, heal, and shelter us and all creatures on Earth. A diminishing biodiversity threatens all life on the planet. In New York City alone, it is estimated that five hundred species of native flora have disappeared since 1800. No other institution in the city does a better job of advocating for the plant world than the New York Botanical Garden (NYBG). With more than a million plants and fifty specialty gardens spread out over 250 acres, it is not only a world-class museum of living plants but also a research and education institution with the important mission of protecting the planet's biodiversity.

Endangered native species of the New York region, along with nearly seven hundred other species, are preserved in the three-and-a-half-acre Native Plant Garden, which celebrates the beauty, diversity, and ecological importance of native flora of the Northeast. The NYBG is also home to thirty thousand notable trees, some more than two hundred years old. A majestic tulip tree predates the garden and inspired the planting of the Tulip Tree Allée that borders the lawn leading to the LuEsther T. Mertz Library. Magnificent specimens of American elm stand tall with their heavy branches outstretched, hallowed relics from another time when these giants ruled the landscape.

Traces of the largest remnant of the forest that blanketed the region upon Henry Hudson's arrival linger within the garden's fifty-acre Thain Family Forest: Lenape hunting trails, glacial striations, ancient trees. The sylvan beauty of this old-growth forest was the primary reason that Nathaniel and Elizabeth Britton—husband-and-wife botanists and founders of the garden—chose this site for the New York Botanical Garden in 1895. Known then as the Hemlock Grove, the forest had remained undeveloped before becoming part of the city's historic acquisition of nearly four thousand acres of new parkland in 1888. Nathaniel Britton described the untouched forest as "the most precious natural possession of the city of New York."

Old-growth forests are established through millennia of ecological changes and continue to evolve as old trees die and new species rise in their place, making up a varied understory. The intrusion of exotic invasive species, human impact, and other environmental factors can quickly disturb this complex ecosystem. The Thain Family Forest has therefore been extensively studied and has managed to preserve its ecologically dense character. Today most of the hemlocks have been decimated by invasive insects. Gone, too, are the forest's chestnuts and elms, but a dense canopy of oaks, tulip trees, American beech, sweet gums, and maples still thrives in the Thain Family Forest, along with an abundance of wildflowers like blue cardinal flower, Canada mayflower, goldenrod, and whitewood aster. Walk along the winding paths, then pause on benches made from fallen ancient trees to meditate on the nature of time and feel the wild beauty of the forest. In summer, its thick canopy provides a cool respite from the heat. Come autumn, the foliage puts on a colorful show.

Whatever the season, the New York Botanical Garden celebrates the wonder and diversity of the plant kingdom. Wide-ranging multimedia exhibitions—such as *Darwin's Garden: An Evolutionary Adventure, Emily Dickinson's Garden:*

established 1891   **total acreage** 250   **entrance** 2900 Southern Boulevard
public transit Bedford Park Blvd **B****D****4** and Allerton Av **2**; Botanical Garden Metro-North
Harlem line   **website** nybg.org

The Peggy Guggenheim Rose Garden

The Poetry of Flowers, and *Kusama: Cosmic Nature*—explore the inextricable connection between plants and human culture. The Enid A. Haupt Conservatory showcases plants from around the world in more than an acre under glass. Soaring palms, prehistoric cycads, and strange cacti fill the conservatory's eleven galleries, each representing a different habitat, from tropical rain forest to arid desert. During the dreary months of winter when the city seems awash in gray, the conservatory is decked out with orchids in a kaleidoscope of shapes and colors, spilling over rocks, dripping on tree trunks, mingling with ferns and moss on the ground. The annual orchid show is not to be missed. It's a chance to be transported to a tropical paradise and indulge in some color therapy when you need it most.

PREVIOUS PAGES, *left*: The Deserts section of the Enid A. Haupt Conservatory; *right*: A colorful display during the annual orchid show. ABOVE: April is the best time to stroll along Magnolia Way.

Spring unfurls across the garden in an explosion of flowering trees and bulbs. Magnolias—the oldest flowering plant on Earth, dating back over 100 million years—are the first to blossom. Ornamental cherries, crab apples, and azaleas follow in quick succession from March to May. Nowhere is the spectacle more immersive than on Daffodil Hill, where the century-old collection of daffodils is naturalized under cherry and crab apple trees. Drifts of daffodils meander down the vast hillside like rivers of white and gold. Just as Wordsworth wrote in his poem, the sight of thousands of daffodils "tossing their heads in a sprightly dance" will fill your heart with pleasure long after you witness it. It's hard to believe that such wondrous nature can be found just a twenty-minute train ride from Grand Central.

ABOVE: Daffodils and crab apples in bloom, a perennial hallmark of spring. FOLLOWING PAGES, *left*: The Bronx River, the only freshwater river in New York City; *right*: Ferns in the Haupt Conservatory.

Bartow–Pell Mansion Garden

A formal garden on a nineteenth-century country estate

Visiting the Bartow–Pell Mansion is like taking a step back in time. Nestled in the sprawling Pelham Bay Park, the estate harks back to the nineteenth century, when the area was a country retreat dotted with gracious mansions.

Like many of the properties in the area at the time, the Bartow–Pell Mansion was once surrounded by pastures, farmland, marshes, and woodland along the shores of Long Island Sound. Near the house were orchards, gardens, and lawns sloping down to the bay, with sweeping views of the water. Pelham Bay once boasted twenty-eight mansions, and Bartow–Pell is the only one that survived New York parks commissioner Robert Moses's demolition spree in the 1930s.

The history of Bartow–Pell goes back to 1654, when Thomas Pell, an English physician from Connecticut, signed a treaty with the Siwanoy people for about fifty thousand acres of land stretching from what is now the Bronx to lower Westchester County. By the end of the Revolutionary War, the Pell estate had been reduced to 220 acres. In 1836, Robert Bartow, a Pell descendant, bought the land and built the present Greek Revival mansion, which remained in his family until the City of New York purchased the property as part of what would become Pelham Bay Park.

The site sat empty for decades until 1914, when the city leased it to the International Garden Club, founded by New York socialite Zelia Hoffman and English garden writer Alice Martineau. Hoffman's ambitious plans for the property included a vast rose garden in the remains of the apple orchard, to be filled with historical and modern cultivars. World War I put a halt to the project, which was ultimately abandoned. The club did, however, restore the mansion and install a large formal walled garden with a series of descending terraces and a central fountain.

Part of the garden's charm is its seclusion. On most days, the rare visitors are scrutinized by a family of deer. With the adjacent wildflower meadow, an herb and vegetable garden, hiking trails along the waterfront, and views of the bay, this quiet corner of the Bronx still feels like the country retreat it once was in the nineteenth century.

Though not easily accessible by public transport, the Bartow–Pell Mansion Museum and its gardens are a rare beauty in the Bronx, and well worth visiting. In the words of Mayor Fiorello H. La Guardia, who used the mansion as his "summer city hall" during the exceptionally hot months of 1936, New York is a big city, and "it does not all center in Manhattan."

established 1914   total acreage 6   entrance 895 Shore Road   public transit Pelham Bay Park ⑥, then **0045** bus to Shore Road/Bartow-Pell Mansion   website bartowpellmansionmuseum.org

Wave Hill

Intimate gardens with magnificent views of the Palisades

Perched on steep slopes overlooking the Hudson River and the Palisades in the quiet neighborhood of Riverdale, Wave Hill has been a leading light in the world of horticulture since its opening in 1967, yet this plant paradise is one of New York's best-kept secrets.

There is much beauty to enjoy at this twenty-eight-acre horticultural gem, not least of which are the wide-open skies and majestic vistas. Despite the grandeur of its location, the gardens at Wave Hill remain intimate in scale and atmosphere. At its heart is the Flower Garden, originally planted with old-fashioned favorites: roses, peonies, and irises. With the passing years, the plant palette has become increasingly bold and more creative. Every year, entirely new compositions fill the garden's four main beds, each with its own color theme. By early fall, the plantings reach a crescendo, the beds overflowing with dahlias, bishops'-weeds, ornamental sages, and so much more, all teetering on the verge of collapse but poignantly beautiful, backlit by the late-afternoon sun.

The Wild Garden, inspired by the Irish gardener William Robinson's treatise on naturalistic planting, is a rich tapestry of botanical wonders from spring into late autumn. Narrow winding paths weave through the richly textured beds that tumble over the hillsides. Panoramic views of the Hudson River provide the backdrop for the tumult of flowers, grasses, and evergreens.

The elegant conservatory is a welcome sanctuary in winter months. When snow is piled high on the ground, tropical flowers intense in color and fragrance show off their charms in the warmth of the Palm House. Like Emily Dickinson, who only had "to cross the floor [of her Massachusetts greenhouse] to stand in the Spice Isles," New Yorkers simply have to take the train uptown to be in South Africa, where the spider iris (*Ferraria crispa*) and the forest lily (*Veltheimia bracteata*) bloom. The greenhouse's small scale invites close inspection of the plants and flowers, all the better to appreciate their intricate details.

Back outdoors, a half-mile trail winds through eight acres of woodland where spring is announced by a glorious carpet of blue glory-of-the-snow sweeping over the hillsides. Expansive lawns offer front-row seats to fiery sunsets when the garden stays open late in summer. As an arboretum, Wave Hill boasts an impressive collection of mature trees, including a centuries-old elm that is arguably the largest specimen in the city.

This garden of wonders is one of the last remaining country estates that used to dot the vicinity. In the nineteenth century, a railway line made the rural area of what would become Riverdale more accessible. Like many of the summer villas that sprang up at the time, Wave Hill was built on former farmland. The property was enlarged over the years and, at various times, served as home to Theodore Roosevelt, Mark Twain, and Arturo Toscanini. In 1960, the Perkins and Freeman families, the last private owners of the property, donated the estate to the City of New York.

From a private estate to a public garden, Wave Hill has retained both its grandeur and intimacy. Art exhibitions and workshops, guided nature walks, live concerts, and yoga make this New York City landmark an all-year destination.

established 1965   total acreage 28   entrance 4900 Independence Avenue
public transit 231 St ❶, then **Bx7** or **BX10** bus to Henry Hudson Pkwy W/W 246 St;
Riverdale Metro-North **Hudson** line   website wavehill.org

The Palm House
OPPOSITE: The Wild Garden

The Pergola in fall, with a
view to the Palisades

Manhattan

The Battery

A storied waterfront public garden since the days of George Washington

The diary entry read, "At home all day, except taking a walk round the Battery in the afternoon." So wrote George Washington in 1789. The Battery by then had already been the site of much history.

The land around the southern tip of Manhattan was once a rich hunting and fishing ground for the Lenape. It was here that Peter Minuit bartered with them for the purchase of the island known as Mannahatta in 1626 (though they had no concept of landownership, since they considered themselves stewards, not owners, of the land). Fort Amsterdam, built to protect the new settlement, served as the headquarters of the Dutch West India Company until the British took over, renaming it Fort George. After the Revolutionary War, the fort's remains were demolished, paving the way for the Battery to become a public promenade with expansive views of the harbor, where Washington often took his stroll in the afternoon. The site would undergo many more drastic changes, as an immigration center (later moved to Ellis Island), an aquarium, and finally a neglected relic, before becoming the public garden known as the Battery today.

In 1994, encouraged by her friend Elizabeth Barlow Rogers, who had pioneered a model of private and public partnership to revitalize Central Park (see page 55), Warrie Price, a self-defined civic servant, founded a nonprofit conservancy to do the same for the Battery. Working from a 1986 master plan by landscape architect Philip Winslow, she recruited Piet Oudolf to create a series of gardens that would match the scale and amplitude of the park's location. The Dutch plantsman, though relatively unknown in America then, was celebrated in Europe for his ability to elicit powerful emotions with evocative gardens, with an emphasis on the plants' life cycle through the seasons.

The twenty-first-century transformation of the Battery began with the Gardens of Remembrance, dedicated to those who perished on September 11, and to the thousands who survived and fled to safety by boarding the ferries on these shores. Waves of native grasses weave through drifts of flowering perennials to make up a long border along the walkway that edges the water. The tapestry of plants, changing with the light, the weather, and the seasons, is both artfully composed and untamed, formal and wild in equal measures. In spring, the honey scent of sea kale lingers gently in the air. Come summer, the licorice-scented giant hyssop entices hordes of bees and butterflies.

In the Battery Bosque, Oudolf transformed the barren ground underneath the grove of mature London plane trees into a rich carpet of shade-loving plants. Thousands of perennial plants and bulbs are densely woven throughout the four-acre garden. In spring, Virginia bluebells, daffodils, and tulips emerge in a riot of colors under the bare trees. Then come the purple globes of alliums, elegant white peonies, and delicate pink gladiolus, undulating through the knitted textures of foliage, from the cool green hostas to the lacy ocher-colored autumn ferns. Soft sandy paths lined with long curving metal benches meander through this kaleidoscope of colors and fragrance that changes every month. On hot summer days, the trees' canopy offers the largest shady refuge

established 1824 **total acreage** 25 **entrance** Battery Place between West and State Streets
public transit South Ferry **1**, Whitehall St **R** **W**, and Bowling Green **4** **5**; Battery Park City ferry
stop **SG** **website** thebattery.org

in downtown New York, while the spiral fountain gives children a chance to cool off. The Statue of Liberty, standing like a beacon in the harbor, is a constant presence in the landscape. The Bosque has all the intimacy and beauty of a private garden in a large public space.

More than a decade after the creation of the Bosque garden, Piet Oudolf returned to the Battery to design the woodland gardens to complement the SeaGlass Carousel. Here the palette is more restrained, limited to the soft shades of pinks and blues derived from the iridescent carousel fish. Dramatic spires of pale pink and lavender wood betony in summer give way to soft blue asters in the mellow autumn days. As Alfredo Taylor-White, one of the volunteer gardeners, put it, the carousel beds provide "a never-ending flow of colors and textures. A continuous show with no intermission."

ABOVE AND OPPOSITE: The Battery prides itself as "a paradise of plants," with the largest perennial gardens in North America free and open to the public every day. The planting design ensures a succession of beautiful colors and

Oudolf's most recent contribution is the planting around the Battery Bikeway that connects the Hudson River Park to the East River Esplanade. A beautiful collection of trees and shrubs—witch hazel, lilac, eastern redbud, viburnum, winterberry—intricately layered like a tableau vivant of a woodland, envelops the sinuous bike path.

Nearby is the one-acre urban farm that grows vegetables and trees as well as houses an oyster restoration station. Students from across the five boroughs help tend the farm and enjoy the harvest. A playscape opened in 2021, with slides, sandboxes, playhouses, a puppet theater, and a climbing structure embedded in different ecological zones, from riverbed and marsh to meadow, bluff, and dunes, all designed to immerse children in nature as they play.

textures through the seasons. *From left to right*: A carpet of Virginia bluebells in early spring; tall spires of Byzantine gladiolus in late May; 'Hummelo' betony in July; blue asters in autumn.

During Superstorm Sandy, water crested the Battery and a wall of water surged into the south end of the park, burying it under two feet of water. Many of the plants perished, but the following spring, the horticultural team put in seven thousand new plants, carefully selecting salt-tolerant species to ensure the garden's resiliency. Though always varying with the seasons and evolving with time and the changing climate, the Battery remains resplendent throughout the year.

If Central Park is New York's backyard, the Battery is the city's doorstep. Poised at the ever-changing edge of the island, it is a place weighted with history, embraced by the magnificent vista of New York Harbor and twenty-five acres of verdant beauty. As Herman Melville wrote, "the battery, where that noble mole is washed by waves, and cooled by breezes, which a few hours previous were out of sight of land. Look at the crowds of water-gazers there."

ABOVE: The SeaGlass Carousel was built in homage to the nineteenth-century New York Aquarium, once housed in Castle Clinton. OPPOSITE: Hostas in bloom in the Bosque gardens.

The Church of St. Luke in the Fields

A welcoming walled garden

Some of New York's most intimate green spaces are the secluded gardens of the city's oldest churches. At the Church of St. Luke in the Fields, the magic of the garden lies well hidden behind its brick walls.

A narrow iron gate on Hudson Street is the portal to this secret garden, one that brings to mind Frances Hodgson Burnett's classic novel. Intersecting paths radiate from a central yellowwood tree and wrap around the perimeter. A circle of benches anchors the center of the garden. More benches are tucked into quiet corners under the shade of green boughs. Flower beds line the paths. The din of the city fades away, muted by the foliage, flowers, and birdsong. In spring, tulips bloom in bright colors. A shower of cherry blossoms blows in the breeze. Pansies show their cheerful faces in ornate planters raised on pedestals.

The church, located between Barrow and Christopher Streets, was built in 1821, when this part of the island lay outside of the city, surrounded by farms, streams, and tree-covered country lanes. What is now the West Village was not yet expanded by landfill, and the church stood at the edge of the Hudson River. In the late eighteenth and early nineteenth centuries, a series of yellow fever epidemics plagued the city, and many New Yorkers sought refuge in the area's country air. The church was named after the patron saint of physicians, an evocation of the Village's role as a sanctuary from pestilence. In the two centuries since its consecration, the church has weathered two destructive fires and more epidemics, including the AIDS pandemic of the 1980s, which affected the congregation deeply. In the last decades, the church has pioneered several programs dedicated to improving the lives of both LGBTQ+ youth and seniors.

In keeping with its welcoming atmosphere, the church has long opened its lush garden to the public. The Barrow Street Garden, as it is formally known, began in 1842 with the first planting of a cutting taken from England's Glastonbury thorn, the legendary tree at a sacred Christian site. (The twice-flowering hawthorn survived until it was blown over in a storm in 1990.) The gardens were expanded in the 1950s when buildings on the site were razed, and then again in 1985, making them the neighborhood's destination for a restorative respite. For New Yorkers enduring the most recent pandemic, the formal walled garden of St. Luke's has provided a peaceful refuge. The benches have been more occupied of late, but the garden remains serene, allowing nature to provide a tonic for hard-pressed city dwellers.

On a hot July day, a whirl of butterflies—tiger swallowtails, admirals, painted ladies, mourning cloaks, skippers—flutters among the flower beds, a blur of wings as colorful and distinctive as those names suggest. Within these ivy-clad walls, the world becomes as described in Burnett's *The Secret Garden*: "Everything is made out of magic, leaves and trees, flowers and birds, badgers and foxes and squirrels and people. So it must be all around us. In this garden—in all the places."

established 1842   **total acreage** 0.7   **entrance** 487 Hudson Street
public transit Christopher St ❶   **website** stlukeinthefields.org

Madison Square Park

A green oasis from the Gilded Age with thought-provoking contemporary art

Madison Square Park, named after the country's fourth president, James Madison, and wedged between two iconic landmarks of New York City—the Flatiron Building on its southern edge and the Empire State Building farther north—has a distinctive history of its own. It is where Theodore Roosevelt and Edith Wharton grew up. Herman Melville and Mark Twain strolled its grounds. O. Henry made the park the backdrop for many of his short stories. Today it is more than an oasis of green and calm amid the concrete delirium of Manhattan; the park has also come to serve as a stage for some of the city's best public art, performances, and pop-up food events.

Designated a public space as far back as 1686, it was first used as a hunting ground, then as a potter's field until 1797. In the nineteenth century, the land was home to an army arsenal, a parade ground, then a house for delinquents before it was made into a park (in truth, little more than a large lawn). In 1870, the west side of the park was shrunk to widen Broadway, but the whole place got a redesign with elegant formal lawns, tree-lined curving paths, and a large fountain. By the end of the twentieth century, however, the park had deteriorated to the point of having "more dirt than green," as described by the *New York Times*. In 1997, a coalition of neighboring businesses and the City Parks Foundation launched a four-year effort to restore Madison Square Park to its nineteenth-century splendor.

Today the Madison Square Park Conservancy maintains this green haven with an ambitious program of community outreach, including gardening workshops, artist's talks, scavenger hunts, garden and wildlife walks, ecological horticulture, and public art. With just over six acres, the park is home to a collection of three hundred trees, including two magnificent centuries-old English elms dating back to the park's beginning. A red oak tree transplanted from James Madison's estate in Virginia in 1936 throws its shade on the Sol LeWitt Lawn on the east side of the park. Red-tailed hawks and American kestrels have recently made their home atop the venerable giants in this urban forest.

With their spidery and fragrant flowers, over seventy varieties of witch hazel brighten up the colder days of fall and winter. Spring is heralded by the emergence of daffodils, the official flower of New York City. Forty-three varieties were planted as part of the Daffodil Project, a citywide initiative to honor the victims of September 11. Thousands of colorful tulips are orchestrated to bloom in a spectacular display, banishing all thoughts of winter. Clouds of white, pink, purple, and pale blue hydrangeas brighten the park from June until August.

On sunny summer days, Madison Square Park is one of the city's most popular destinations. Children shriek their way through the water fountains to cool off or sing along to the music of the kids' concert series. The line for Shake Shack wraps around the block all day long, and diners linger into the evening under strings of lights. The Oval Lawn, at the heart of the park, is a magnet for sunbathers, picnickers, and city dwellers enjoying a relaxing moment in their hectic day. It is also the setting for some of the most thought-provoking public art in the city, including Maya Lin's 2021

established 1847 **total acreage** 6.2 **entrance** 11 Madison Avenue **public transit** 23 St Ⓡ Ⓦ ❻
website madisonsquarepark.org

Ghost Forest, an installation of forty-nine towering Atlantic white cedars dying from damages caused by saltwater infiltration in their natural habitat, a haunting reminder of the climate crisis.

With its long and winding history, Madison Square Park is pointing the way to what a city park can be in the twenty-first century. This urban haven gives all New Yorkers access to a green space that allows for more than just recreation and respite. As the only Level II arboretum— a collection of more than one hundred species, varieties, or cultivars of trees and woody plants— in Manhattan, the park aims to restore the city's urban jungle, reviving local ecosystems that will sustain residents and visitors visually, artistically, and environmentally.

ABOVE: A Kwanzan cherry tree in bloom. OPPOSITE: The park boasts more than seventy-five hydrangea cultivars, which bloom from June to August.

Central Park

The people's park

Central Park is arguably the crown jewel of parks in New York City, a miraculous rectangle of emerald green at the heart of a gray metropolis. Against the background of a rapidly growing, industrialized New York, Frederick Law Olmsted and Calvert Vaux designed Central Park as a sylvan counterpoint to the bustle of the city, offering urban dwellers rich and poor alike a chance to commune with nature. Olmsted called the park *rus in urbe*, "country in the city" in Latin. Its construction was a massive undertaking, a feat of complex engineering to remodel the topography of a denuded forest into a series of gentle hills and dales, dense woodlands and open meadows, areas of wilderness and formal plazas. Water sources were redirected and pipes were laid to create meandering streams, cascading waterfalls, and calming lakes. Millions of trees and plants were put into the ground, artfully arranged to convey the illusion of an unbounded pastoral landscape. Thousands of workers were employed, including the city's burgeoning immigrant population—Irish laborers, Italian artisans, and German gardeners.

As Witold Rybczynski observed in his biography of Olmsted, "for mid-nineteenth-century Americans, Central Park really was a magical place. Not just a pretty setting for recreation, it was an aesthetic experience." Walt Whitman thought the park was at its best during the month of May, when he visited "almost every day, sitting, or slowly rambling, or riding around." Henry James noted that while there are greater sights in the world, to be in Central Park was "to be thrilled at every turn." More than just a park, Olmsted and Vaux's masterpiece is New York City's largest work of art. Robert Smithson, who pioneered the land art movement in the 1960s, deemed Olmsted America's first "earthwork artist."

When Robert Moses, the Parks Department commissioner from 1934 to 1960, took charge of Central Park, it had suffered badly from years of neglect. Unlike Olmsted, who had envisioned the park as a place of rest and contemplation, Moses believed it should be a place of recreation and activity, sacrificing scenery in favor of facilities such as ball fields, playgrounds, and parking lots. Nonetheless, Moses was responsible for the park's first and only formal garden. Named the Conservatory Garden, it was created on the site of a nursery with a large complex of glass greenhouses, built in 1899. It was a major tourist attraction with its then-exotic tropical plants and ornate flower beds, but at the height of the Depression, it was deemed too expensive to maintain and was demolished. The formal garden as we know it today was built as a WPA project, financed by FDR's New Deal. In the 1970s, like the rest of Central Park, the Conservatory Garden deteriorated into a wasteland. The flower beds were filled with garbage, the trees overgrown, and the stone walls covered in graffiti. In 1982, determined to bring it back to life, Elizabeth Rogers, leader of the newly formed Central Park Conservancy, enlisted her painter friend Lynden Miller, who raised the funds for the restoration herself. Reopened in 1987 with Miller's new planting design, the garden was resurrected with myriad flowers and shrubs, carefully orchestrated

established 1858   total acreage 843   entrances Along Central Park West, North 110th Street, 59th Street, 8th Avenue, and 5th Avenue   public transit Ⓐ Ⓒ Ⓑ Ⓓ between 59 St–Columbus Circle and Cathedral Pkwy, Ⓝ Ⓠ Ⓡ Ⓦ between 57 St–7 Ave and 59 St, 59 St–Columbus Circle ❶, and Central Park North ❷❸   website centralparknyc.org

into a nonstop show from spring through fall. (Such was her success that Miller went on to reshape many of the city's public spaces, including Bryant Park, Madison Square Park, and Wagner Park in Battery Park City.)

The six-acre garden is divided into three sections: a French-style North Garden, an Italianate Center Garden, and an English-style South Garden. The garden's formal design is signaled at its main entrance on Fifth Avenue by an imposing and ornate wrought-iron gate. Made in Paris in 1894, it once guarded the Vanderbilt mansion at Fifth Avenue and Fifty-Eighth Street.

Down the steps from the gate is the Center Garden, a symmetrical design influenced by Italian Renaissance gardens. A sweeping green lawn is bordered on the north and south sides by yew hedges and twin allées of mature crab apple

ABOVE AND OPPOSITE, *from left to right*: A dedicated "rustic crew" builds and maintains the park's many rustic features; the sculpture *Angel of the Waters* was the first public art commission in New York City to be given to a

trees, originally grown upstate and brought to the city by barges on the Hudson. In spring, a canopy of frothy white and pink blossoms hangs over the wooden benches. A geyser fountain stands between the western edge of the lawn and a semicircular pergola draped in purple wisteria blooms whose perfume drifts beyond the garden gate down Fifth Avenue, drawing in passersby.

In the North Garden, French parterres in knotted designs encircle the Untermyer Fountain, featuring the *Three Dancing Maidens* by the German sculptor Walter Schott. On the surrounding sloping beds, twenty thousand blooming tulips announce the arrival of spring, while autumn is celebrated with two thousand Korean chrysanthemums. Both are breathtaking markers of the seasons.

woman, Emma Stebbins; an early-spring stroll through the park; Gapstow Bridge over the Pond. FOLLOWING PAGES: The entrance to the Conservatory Garden's English-style garden.

The South Garden, in the style of an English perennial garden, is the most intimate of the three sections. Arranged in concentric planting beds around the Burnett Fountain's water lily pool, the garden is animated by a succession of blooms from the magnificent magnolias in early spring to the hardy perennials that flower from summer to late fall. With benches tucked behind tall hedges and lilac-scented walkways, the English garden offers itself as every New Yorker's private garden. The three distinct but equally transporting sections of the Conservatory Garden make it a hidden gem within the crown jewel.

Olmsted and Vaux's ingenious design made Central Park an enduring work of art that is also a monument to the democratic ideals of nineteenth-century America. In Olmsted's words, it is "the people's park." New Yorkers of all ages have claimed

ABOVE, *left*: The Burnett Fountain, a memorial for the author of *The Secret Garden*, Frances Hodgson Burnett; *right*: a bench under a lilac tree in the English-style garden.

this immensely rich, multilayered public preserve as their own—bird-watchers, horticulturalists, historians, dancers, skaters, ballplayers, runners, readers, flaneurs. In the century and a half since its creation, Central Park has held the affection of not just local citizens but also of millions of tourists who come from all over the world to admire its beauty. They are joined by generations of birds and waterfowl who stop by during their yearly migration to enjoy the park's dense woodlands, limpid lakes, and lush lawns. The park also has its permanent denizens: hawks, herons, woodpeckers, thrushes, a bald eagle, a coyote. Others, like the magical snowy owl that showed up in early 2021—the first visit by the species in more than 130 years—stay long enough to keep New Yorkers enthralled before moving on, presumably to colder climes. There is enough magic in Central Park for everyone.

ABOVE, *left*: The fountain in the center Italian-style garden; *right*: the crab apple allée in bloom. FOLLOWING PAGES: The multicolored chrysanthemums in the French-style garden are an annual fall highlight.

The Central Park Lake in the snow

The Heather Garden at Fort Tryon Park

A poetic garden with commanding views over the Hudson River

"This site gives one of the most magnificent views in the world . . . I know no landscape near a big city that takes the breath away more completely," wrote the *New Yorker* architecture critic Lewis Mumford of Fort Tryon Park and its dramatic vistas of the Hudson River and the Palisades—the majestic escarpment rising to 540 feet above the water on the New Jersey side. Built into a rocky ledge within this rugged landscape is one of the city's most beautiful flower gardens, the Heather Garden.

Fort Tryon Park sits on land once inhabited by the Wecquaesgeek, one of the last Lenape nations to be driven out of Mannahatta. During the Revolutionary War, American forces suffered one of the worst defeats on these hills, and the victorious British renamed the fortifications Fort Tryon, after the last governor of colonial New York. Though much of the forest was cut down during the Revolutionary War, Washington Heights, as it became known, remained a sylvan haven through the end of the nineteenth century, enticing wealthy New Yorkers looking to build country retreats. In 1917, John D. Rockefeller Jr. bought three of the largest properties in the area, which he immediately offered to the city. "All my life I have thought of what a fine park this land would make," wrote Rockefeller in 1917. It would take eighteen years, a fortune, and much tenacity to realize his vision.

For the design of the park, Rockefeller turned to Frederick Law Olmsted Jr., son of Central Park's codesigner. Olmsted's design embraced the steep rocky topography, preserving its natural beauty while cutting eight miles of winding paths through the land, carving out small open lawns, and adding hundreds of mature trees, including native species that once grew in forests from the days of the Wecquaesgeek: ashes, hickories, sassafrases, beeches, laurels, hemlocks, and tulip trees. Olmsted created terraces at different levels to frame the panoramic views of the Hudson and the Palisades with changing foregrounds, "some intricate and intimate, some grandiose and simple, some richly architectural or gardenesque, some picturesquely naturalistic," as he wrote in his preliminary report of 1927.

The Heather Garden, with its three acres sited on the grounds of an early-twentieth-century estate, was designed to embody the gardenesque element of the park. Building into the side of the rocky ridge, Olmsted set out a series of terraces along a promenade lined with elm trees. A lengthy central path divides the garden into two large flower beds. A perennial border with a profusion of flowers is planted east of the path. In the rocky west-facing bed, Olmsted chose heaths and heathers, whose low-growing habits would not obstruct the views of the Hudson River.

Much of Olmsted's original design was subsequently compromised, first through an ill-conceived renovation in 1955, then through decades of neglect. In 1983, the Greenacre Foundation, founded by Rockefeller's daughter Abby Rockefeller Mauzé, funded a restoration of Fort Tryon Park, including a complete rehabilitation of the Heather Garden to bring it closer to Olmsted's original design, with new plantings to extend bloom time. Invasive Norway and sycamore maple trees were removed. Elsewhere, overgrown trees were replaced with smaller specimens to reclaim the views.

established 1935   **total acreage** 3   **entrance** 741 Fort Washington Avenue
public transit 190 St Ⓐ   **website** forttryonparktrust.org

The garden was reinvigorated once again ahead of its seventy-fifth anniversary. Lynden Miller and Ronda Brands were engaged to update the plantings, with a framework plan to ensure the long-term preservation of the garden. Through the two renovations, a stately Siberian elm that likely took root in the middle of the heather bed was left to spread its canopy over a tapestry of hostas. Consulting Olmsted's original planting list, the designers refined the plant selection, swapping out invasive varieties with others that share a similar shape, texture, and color. Japanese barberry was replaced with a dwarf smoke bush cultivar, a deutzia, or an abelia. Native species like hummingbird mint and butterfly weed were added to attract pollinators and increase diversity. The garden, as Brands suggests, "is a poem written over time."

ABOVE AND OPPOSITE: The Heather Garden is especially spectacular in fall. *From left to right*: The bronze foliage of an oak tree backlit by the afternoon sun; a center path divides the garden into a perennial border (on the *left*)

While constantly evolving, the Heather Garden retains its splendor through all seasons. In spring, a carpet of bluebells is punctuated with the bright colors of azaleas and rhododendrons while lilacs, daphne, and peonies perfume the air. Summer brings a riot of blooms from roses, clematis, hydrangeas, hardy hibiscus, yarrows, and mock oranges. In autumn, the foliage puts on a spectacular show of colors. As winter gives way to spring, the blooming heaths cut an undulating swath of pink and white through the heather beds. No matter the time of year, the garden is vibrant with colors and textures, drawing plant lovers of all kinds, including birds, bees, butterflies, and other beneficial wildlife. More than a century since Rockefeller articulated his vision for this land, Fort Tryon remains one of the city's finest parks.

and heather bed (on the *right*); dwarf abelia in bloom; the rich carpet of plantings under the elm tree. FOLLOWING PAGES: The winter heaths in bloom.

The Met Cloisters

Medieval architecture, art, and gardens on the rocky summit of Fort Tryon Park

The crowning feature of Fort Tryon Park, the Met Cloisters enfolds within its fortress walls some of the most uniquely beautiful gardens in the city. Perhaps one of the greatest gifts to New York City, it is the culmination of John D. Rockefeller Jr.'s two-decade effort to create Fort Tryon Park and to fulfill his vision of a museum of medieval art.

It began with the Metropolitan Museum of Art's purchase—funded by Rockefeller—in 1925 of the sculptor George Grey Barnard's collection of medieval art and architecture fragments. For the next twelve years, Rockefeller commissioned design studies for a new building to house the collection, sponsored research trips to the South of France for the architect Charles Collens to study medieval architecture, and helped purchase a great number of medieval treasures for the new museum. From his own collection, Rockefeller donated the magnificent series of seven "Hunt of the Unicorn" tapestries, some of the most beautiful surviving works of art from the Middle Ages. Built with the help of a WPA workforce, the Cloisters finally opened to the public in May 1938.

Designed as a fortified monastery, the museum is centered around four Romanesque and Gothic cloisters reconstructed from fragments of various monasteries in France and Spain. A cloister—a covered walkway surrounding a large courtyard open to the air—formed the heart of monasteries in the Middle Ages. Secluded and private yet filled with light and greenery, the medieval cloisters were ideal places for peaceful meditation. At the Cloisters, the gardens in the open courtyards were developed by two medieval art scholars: James Rorimer, the museum's first director, and Margaret Freeman, a lecturer and

Rorimer's successor. Drawing from medieval texts and illustrated herbals, they composed an extensive plant list that continues to be developed and amplified. Gardeners at the Cloisters through the years have thus been able to fill the gardens with plants that make the medieval world depicted in the museum's tapestries, stained glass, paintings, and decorative works of art come to life.

Of the eighty-three species of plants identified in the Unicorn Tapestries, fifty of them are planted at various times of the year in the Trie Cloister garden. The planting mimics the millefleur style of some of the tapestries, where the flowers are depicted in a flat, dense, and carpet-like background. In the garden, columbines, lady's mantle, daisies, cornflowers, feverfew, carnations, wild strawberries, forget-me-nots, orchids, sweet violets, and wild fennel grow in an impenetrable mass under holly, medlar, and orange trees.

The Bonnefont Cloister, on a terrace overlooking the Hudson River, contains an herb garden planted exclusively with species known in the Middle Ages. While the Trie Cloister garden is a fantasy, the herb garden offers a glimpse of what such gardens might have looked like in monastic and secular communities centuries ago. Organized in separate raised beds around a fifteenth-century Venetian wellhead are over 250 species of plants used for culinary, medicinal, aromatic, artistic, and even magical purposes. The bed for dye plants features the three species used to create the glorious array of colors in the Unicorn Tapestries: madder, whose roots produce a red; woad, whose leaves yield a blue; and weld, from whose leaves, stems, and seeds a yellow is extracted. The bright yellow stigmas of saffron

established 1938 **total acreage** 4 **entrance** 99 Margaret Corbin Drive
public transit Dyckman St Ⓐ **website** metmuseum.org

were once a source of gold substitute. Today saffron is planted along with celandine in the bed reserved for artistic uses. Combining the yellow juice of celandine with egg yolk and mercury, medieval artists created an alternative for gold leaf used in illuminated manuscripts.

The Cuxa Cloister garden, all flowery abundance around a central fountain, is a pleasure garden with intimations of paradise.

Plants are chosen for their beauty and fragrance, though not strictly limited to those known in the Middle Ages. Intersecting paths divide the garden into four quadrants, each anchored by a tree: a crab apple, a pear, a hawthorn, and a cornelian cherry. Tulips, daffodils, and grape hyacinths herald spring, followed by a procession of blooms that carries on until late autumn, ensured by the inclusion of bleeding hearts, astilbes, anemones,

PREVIOUS PAGES: The Cuxa Cloister in spring. ABOVE AND OPPOSITE: The Bonnefont Cloister Herb Garden. *From left to right*: A Venetian limestone wellhead; columbines and roses in the Love and Fertility Bed; wattle fences,

and asters. Stone benches in the adjacent chapter house where eight hundred years ago Cistercian and Benedictine monks once sat provide a quiet place to contemplate the ephemeral beauty of flowers and their eternal appeal.

Just as the medieval cloisters were once the still center of monastic life where the calamities of the world were kept at bay, the sense of harmony, peace, and timelessness in the gardens at the Met Cloisters offers a retreat from the clamorous demands of the modern world. Make the pilgrimage to this remote hilltop and you will experience medieval life in the heart of twenty-first-century Manhattan. As Jorge Luis Borges, the Argentine author of genre-bending fiction, poetry, and essays, wrote in his poem about the museum, "time in this place does not obey an order."

a common feature of medieval gardens; foxgloves in the Medicinal Bed. FOLLOWING PAGES, *left*: The Trie Cloister; *right*: An espalier pear tree planted in the 1940s.

Paley Park

An urban treasure in miniature

Paley Park, New York's best-known vest-pocket park, is a miniscule haven that has had an enduring influence on the city's public spaces. Tucked away on East Fifty-Third Street between Madison and Fifth Avenues, the one-tenth-acre lot was donated by William Paley, the then chairman of CBS, to create the park as a memorial to his father. With an ingeniously simple design, Paley and the team of architects at Zion & Breen Associates gave New Yorkers a peaceful walled garden amid the bustle of Midtown Manhattan and a prototype for compact urban green spaces.

At the heart of the park is an imposing twenty-foot-high waterfall, reaching across the entire north end, purifying the air while drowning out the noises of the city with its crashing water. Dense evergreen ivy smothers the walls on either side, enveloping the space in its verdant embrace. A grove of honey locusts, their foliage changing with the seasons, juxtaposes nature's ebb and flow against the unyielding buildings that mark the park's boundaries. Lacy foliage filters the harsh summer sun into gently dappled shade. In November, the leaves become a golden canopy that glows in the autumn light. By December, they disappear altogether to make room for the warming winter sun. A changing parade of colorful flowers winds through the year, held in containers scattered around the seating area. Marble tables and movable chairs give users both comfort and control over their experience of the space.

Like a tiny forest clearing, Paley Park draws busy office workers and harried tourists alike to take refuge in its calming atmosphere. Workers gather to eat their lunch in the shade of the honey locusts; others sit to contemplate the falling water, letting the bustle of the street fall away.

The concept of vest-pocket parks can be traced back to the late nineteenth century, championed by Jacob Riis, a pioneering photojournalist and urban reformer who encouraged New Yorkers to reimagine overlooked spaces, however small, as much-needed oases of green space in the urban morass that Manhattan had become. Thomas Hoving, appointed New York parks commissioner by Mayor John Lindsay in 1966, saw vest-pocket parks as the best way to serve different communities, declaring that "utopia would mean a park—some large, some small—every four or five blocks." In his version of utopia, vacant lots and abandoned buildings would be transformed into a network of small parks—a thousand of them, to be exact, from tiny playgrounds to large community gardens. At the same time, Lindsay took advantage of a 1961 zoning resolution to encourage "private developers to provide spaces for the public within or outside their buildings" in exchange for zoning concessions, ushering in a new form of privately owned public spaces (POPS), beginning with the opening of Paley Park in 1967.

The park remains one of Manhattan's treasures, inspiring city park designers around the world. The urbanist William H. Whyte made it one of the subjects of his seminal study *The Social Life of Small Urban Spaces*, which in turn influenced the successful rehabilitation of Bryant Park.

Today New York has 590 POPS of various shapes and sizes, both outdoor and indoor, making nearly ninety acres of private space— the equivalent of nine Bryant Parks—accessible to the public in the various boroughs. In a city where close to nine million people are crammed into less than four hundred square miles, no patch of green is too small or inconsequential.

established 1967   **total acreage** 0.1   **entrance** 3 East 53rd Street
public transit 5 Av/53 St 🄴 🄼   **website** paleypark.org

Albert's Garden

Punk rock, street art, and flowers

Albert's Garden, a small community garden on a quiet block in the East Village, is a peaceful reminder of a heady time in New York. Punk rock venue CBGB was located around the corner on the Bowery, and the Ramones posed for their 1976 album cover against a brick wall on the west side of the garden.

Befitting its punk rock cred, the garden had a DIY start. Located at 16–18 East Second Street, between the Bowery and Second Avenue, the site originally housed two brownstones repossessed by the City of New York for unpaid taxes. When the houses were condemned and torn down in 1968, a basketball court was built in their place. Not much basketball was played there. Within a few years, it became a trash heap.

Then came Albert Eisenlau Jr. In 1973, the antiques dealer, who lived at 10 East Second Street, began cleaning up the site, hauling out broken-down refrigerators, tin cans, and bottles. Soon he was joined by two neighbors, the sculptor Louise Kruger and the painter Ben Wohlberg. Together they dug up the asphalt to make way for a garden. The trio was resourceful in finding materials and supplies for their endeavor. As Kruger recalled in an interview with Grace Tankersley in 2009, "Early on it was a bit of an adventure in many ways." Plants were procured through donations or by trading, and "anywhere there was a giveaway, we'd hop along," she added. A sculptor friend of Kruger's donated the initial soil from her earthwork installation in a gallery. Eisenlau planted many of the mature trees that now grace the garden. A peach tree—now replaced by an apple tree—grew from a pit that Eisenlau had thrown into a garbage pile. Other trees, including three mulberries and a locust, grew from seeds brought by the birds. Roses, peonies, hydrangeas, and hellebores were some of the flowers planted early on. Wohlberg dug a pond and made the curving paths around the garden. Kruger set up a working studio in one section, carving her sculptures from wood and using the shavings to mulch the paths.

During the next two decades, community gardens like Albert's flourished in many of the city's low-income neighborhoods. Kruger recalled "a lot of cooperation between the gardens in terms of things that were needed." The city allowed volunteers to maintain the gardens—as long as they kept them open to the public—as a means to combat urban blight. They provided much-needed green spaces. The Parks Department initiated the GreenThumb community gardens organization to lead horticultural workshops and provide material support.

Despite their success at rehabilitating the neighborhoods, the gardens' existence was often precarious. In 1989, the city put many of the community gardens, including Albert's, on the auction block. Kruger galvanized garden members to call everyone they knew. Eventually, word reached the mayor's office, and on the day of the auction, a black limo pulled up in front of the garden and Mayor Ed Koch stuck his head out of the window and looked around briefly. At the end of the day, the garden was taken off the auction block. In 1998, the garden was at risk once again when Mayor Rudy Giuliani wanted to sell 114 of the city's community gardens to developers. Kruger, along with other garden members, joined the citywide protest and testified at City Hall in

established 1973   total acreage 0.07   entrance 16–18 East 2nd Street
public transit 2 Av Ⓕ   website albertsgarden.org

the effort to stop the sale. Fortunately, the Trust for Public Land, along with Bette Midler's New York Restoration Project, stepped in and saved all the gardens, ensuring their existence in perpetuity.

Today Albert's Garden is a shady oasis that hosts events including poetry readings, art installations, and a Halloween party to close out the year. A large bird mural by the Belgian street artist ROA greets visitors at the gate. Albert Eisenlau passed away in 1986, having left the city years before. Ben Wohlberg moved to Block Island to continue painting. Louise Kruger carried on looking after the garden, with the help of volunteers and new members, until her death in 2013. Their creative spirit—and a slice of history of the East Village— lives on for future generations at the garden.

ABOVE: Mulberry trees provide a shady respite on hot summer days. OPPOSITE: The sculptural redbud (*left*) planted by Albert Eisenlau Jr. is a signature tree of the garden.

Liz Christy Community Garden

New York City's first official community garden and the birthplace of the Green Guerillas

For New Yorkers in the 1960s and '70s, gardening was a radical act of urban conservation. Hobbled by a fiscal crisis and widespread disinvestment, the city was a prime example of urban decay. Blocks after blocks of buildings were abandoned or left in a state of disrepair, especially in poorer neighborhoods. In the face of neglect, people took matters into their own hands and set out to transform their environment through gardening.

The busy corner of Houston and the Bowery was once the southern tip of a large farm owned by Peter Stuyvesant, the last Dutch governor of New Amsterdam. By the time Liz Christy moved into her art studio three blocks away in the early 1970s, the corner lot had sat empty for decades, filled with trash several feet deep. One day, as she walked by, a young boy was playing amid the rubble, climbing in an upturned refrigerator. She decided that something needed to change. Christy saw the land's nurturing potential under the debris of urban blight. Spurred by the idea that the site could be a garden—as a reminder of the farmland it once was and a place for the growth of communities—she gathered a dozen friends and neighbors to help her realize this pioneering vision of urban green space.

It took the group, mostly young college students with hardly any horticultural knowledge, six months, working every weekend, just to clean up the lot. What they created together was a twentieth-century farm and garden firmly rooted in its urban environment. Christy laid out the basic paths—all curvilinear to counter the rigid city grid—and distributed the plots to all who requested one, reserving a plot for children. She also procured donations of plants and shrubs from

the Farm and Garden Nursery on Reade Street. Fertilizer came in the form of horse manure from the police stable at the other end of West Houston Street. Water was siphoned from a nearby fire hydrant. A wood arbor was built by public high school students of one of the gardeners. Corn, herbs, pumpkins, and sunflowers flourished in communal plots for the consumption of everyone. In the private plots, the vegetables were as diverse as the gardeners: Chinese cabbage, Italian and Spanish beans, collard greens, and black-eyed peas. As Christy told a reporter from the *Daily News*, "People have shared recipes with one another from their ethnic heritages," adding that a local unhoused man "wrote down a delicious recipe for fried squash flowers."

The Bowery Houston Community Farm and Garden was officially recognized by the Parks Department as the city's first community garden in 1974, and the gardeners were given a one-dollar monthly lease for the land. By then, Christy and her friends had started to call themselves the Green Guerillas, greening the city through unconventional tactics. They threw "seed green-aids" into vacant lots, planted flower window boxes in abandoned buildings, sowed sunflowers in the center meridians of busy streets, and helped others start their own community gardens. They held gardening workshops and organized plant donations. Over the next decade, more than a thousand community gardens sprouted in the five boroughs.

Liz Christy passed away in 1985, and the Bowery Houston Community Farm and Garden was renamed in her honor a year later. Today twenty dedicated members look after the Liz

established 1974   **total acreage** 0.26   **entrance** East Houston Street between Second Avenue and the Bowery   **public transit** 2nd Av Ⓕ   **website** lizchristygarden.us

Christy Community Garden, where her green spirit continues to grow. The first tree planted, a dawn redwood (an ancient species from the days of the dinosaurs) sapling donated by the New York Botanical Garden, is now a giant, the largest specimen in Manhattan. The shady canopy from the trees has made growing vegetables no longer viable, but on the eastern end of the garden is a mini orchard, with fruit trees bearing plums, peaches, and figs in summer, along with a native pawpaw tree that recently started fruiting after twenty years. In spring, a flowering cherry tree near the entrance blankets the garden in pink blossoms. Flowers bloom in profusion from early spring to late fall. A koi pond is also the permanent home of red-eared slider turtles. Even while traffic roars outside its fences, the garden is a tranquil oasis, with benches in

PREVIOUS PAGES: The garden reaches its peak in abundance and lushness in October. ABOVE AND OPPOSITE, *from left to right*: Ivy climbing up the magnolia tree; garden residents include koi fish, as well as red-eared slider

hidden corners enveloped in climbing vines and fragrant roses.

By simply making a garden, with flowers and vegetables grown in sixty raised beds, Liz Christy left a transformative legacy. Today there remain more than 550 community gardens in the city, with the greatest concentration in the East Village, including the Green Oasis Community Garden and Carmen Pabón del Amanecer Jardín, where

the first generation of Nuyorican poets performed and honed their voices. As the writer Rebecca Solnit posits in her insightful book *Orwell's Roses*, "nature itself is immensely political, in how we imagine, interact with, and impact it." Nearly five decades after its formation, the Green Guerillas continue to give New Yorkers who need it most access to nature and agency in the shaping of their environment.

turtles; Liz Christy laid out winding paths throughout the garden, creating secluded seating corners like this one; the splendor of spring: cherry blossoms in April.

Jefferson Market Garden

A Greenwich Village gem on the site of a former women's prison

Sitting behind an elegant wrought-iron fence on the corner of Sixth and Greenwich Avenues is Jefferson Market Garden, a haven of unhurried charm amid the whirl of traffic. An abundance of flowering trees enfolds an oval central lawn. Magnolia, dogwood, crab apple, and cherry blossoms orchestrate a symphony of pink petals from early April into May. A stately yellowwood tree casts its shade on sunny days through wide-spreading branches. Brick paths lead to bountiful flower beds bursting with colors and scent throughout the seasons. In 1998, a wrought-iron fence and gate, designed to complement the adjacent Jefferson Market Branch of the New York Public Library, replaced the old chain-link fence, thanks to a generous donation from Brooke Astor and the Vincent Astor Foundation.

Every year, the garden throws open its gate in April, when the tulips are blooming, along with daffodils, fritillaries, and grape hyacinths. In June, the rose garden proffers a profusion of blooms swirling around a fountain, climbing over the fence, dripping from a pergola. Dahlias in multicolored hues flower all summer long into the last days of the garden's year. Some of the garden's ardent fans are children, who gravitate toward the koi pond or gather to paint pumpkins at the Fall Harvest Festival. At the Festival of Flowers, they parade through the garden and bop along to live music.

Jefferson Market Garden may now be known as a lush haven in the heart of Greenwich Village, but like many of the city's gardens that sprouted in the 1970s, this oasis was built on the wreckage of a demolished building. The garden owes its appellation to an open farmers' market established in 1833, but it sits on ground that for many years was home to the notorious Women's House of Detention, whose famous inmates included Mae West (for appearing in her show called *Sex*), Ethel Rosenberg (for sharing atomic secrets with the Soviet Union), and Valerie Solanas (for shooting Andy Warhol).

When the jail was demolished in 1974, competing uses for the land were proposed—a nursing home and a parking lot, among others. But garden activists persisted, and the land was transferred to the Parks Department. Through bake sales, book sales, and letter-writing campaigns, volunteers raised the money to make the garden. The Vincent Astor Foundation gave them a start with a contribution.

Early critics were not impressed with the garden that rose from the debris of the Village jail, calling it "pigeon alley." But more than forty years after a group of activists stood on a patch of rubble and declared that the land would be made into a garden for the community, Jefferson Market Garden is beloved by New Yorkers near and far. Like Andy Warhol, who was a frequent visitor, many have sought refuge from the roar of traffic in this tranquil oasis. Weddings and memorials have been held on the lawn. Come stroll around the garden to admire the flowers, listen to the birds, or sit and unwind on one of the benches enveloped in flower beds.

established 1975   **total acreage** 0.4   **entrance** 10 Greenwich Avenue
public transit W 4 St ⒷⒹⒻⓂⒶⒸⒺ   **website** jeffersonmarketgarden.org

West Side Community Garden

Dutch flowers in old Bloomingdale

The land on which the West Side Community Garden now sits was once part of a coastal oak and pine forest, surrounded by picturesque hills, valleys, wetlands, ponds, and streams. The early Dutch settlers named the area Bloemendaal, meaning "valley of flowers" (which later became Bloomingdale when the English took over the island).

The most spectacular time to visit the West Side Community Garden is during the annual Tulip Festival. Held for a week in April, during the flower's peak bloom, the festival draws a crowd from all over the city looking to soak up the tulips' ravishing beauty. Daffodils, scilla, and hyacinths join in the display of nearly one hundred varieties of tulips, planted in concentric beds around a small lawn. Swaths of jewel-toned blooms mixed with striped and brightly hued varieties make up a spectacle as colorful as an artist's paint box.

But the garden also flourishes during the rest of the year, with roses, lilies, irises, peonies, and other flowering perennials blooming in abundance. Movie nights, evening concerts in June, Shakespeare performances, and a Fourth of July barbecue and potluck keep the garden busy with happy visitors all summer long. It is one of the rare privately owned green spaces that is open to the public every day, with all events, except an annual fundraising gala, free of charge. The West Side Community Garden is not just a neighborhood sanctuary. It's a small treasure for the entire city in its embodiment of the colorful history and community spirit of the Upper West Side.

In 1790, the contemporary site of the garden became part of a three-hundred-acre property that included a Palladian mansion, surrounded by orchards and meadows. In the nineteenth century, the mansion became a beer and dance hall and the orchards and meadows gave way to row houses, apartment buildings, and working-class tenements.

The Upper West Side today is known as the home of Lincoln Center and stately apartment buildings like the Dakota, whose famous residents ranged from Rudolf Nureyev and Leonard Bernstein to Lauren Bacall and John Lennon. It's difficult to imagine, but the West Side Community Garden rose out of a neglected lot known as "strip city" because it was a dumping ground for stolen cars that had been stripped of their parts. In 1976, parents whose children walked through the debris-strewn lot between Eighty-Ninth and Ninetieth Streets as a shortcut to school rallied their neighbors and gained access to the land from the city. Together they cleared the garbage and made a flourishing garden of flowers and vegetables.

In 1985, the city approved a development project for the lot and its neighboring plot. With the help of the Trust for Public Land, the gardeners were able to form a nonprofit and negotiate a plan to save part of the garden. The gardeners received a deed in perpetuity, and volunteers have maintained the garden to the enjoyment of all New Yorkers ever since, reminding us that this part of the Upper West Side was once a valley of blooms.

established 1976   total acreage 0.4   entrance 123 West 89th Street between Amsterdam and Columbus Avenues   public transit 86 St ❶   website westsidecommunitygarden.org

The Lotus Garden

A rooftop garden born from the rubble of vaudeville theaters

New York City is full of hidden treasures. Climb the stairs next to a parking garage on Ninety-Seventh Street between Broadway and West End Avenue and you will find the Lotus Garden, the Upper West Side's secret oasis. Sitting atop the parking garage, unseen from street level and hemmed in on three sides by tall buildings, the garden is the happy ending of a long and extraordinary story that embodies the history of the Upper West Side and the resourcefulness of land-starved New Yorkers to claim a place for the simple pleasure of growing some flowers.

This block was once the center of vaudeville, with sumptuous theaters that became the mecca for the movies in the 1940s and the following decades. Yet by 1976, these opulent palaces had been reduced to a heap of rubble. As the sites of the Riviera and Riverside Theatres sat derelict, members of the Ninety-Seventh Street block association persuaded the owner to let them garden on some of the land. Soon flowers were planted, and the newly minted gardeners began calling themselves the Garden People. Word spread that land was being given away on the block, and people came to claim a plot of their own. Within a few years, the garden grew to be a full acre, tended by 125 people in seventy-five plots.

In 1981, however, the idyll came to an end when a new building project was proposed and bulldozers were brought in to raze the gardens. The new parks commissioner, Henry Stern, came to the rescue and gave the Garden People a plot to create a new garden in Riverside Park. (Named the Ninety-First Street Community Garden, it remains a beloved slice of the Upper West Side,

known for its well-tended colorful flower beds. It even made an appearance in the 1998 Tom Hanks and Meg Ryan romantic comedy *You've Got Mail*.)

After impassioned pleas from the Garden People, representatives from the Green Guerillas (see page 87), and organizations ranging from the Trust for Public Land to GreenThumb and the New York Botanical Garden, the developer of the proposed tower on the original site agreed to include a community garden on top of the condominium's parking garage, providing seven thousand square feet of soil, $25,000 for start-up costs, and a $50,000 endowment for the garden's maintenance. Much more was spent in engineering the parking garage to support two and a half feet of soil, two small ponds, and a drainage system. The twenty-eight gardeners divided the space into an equal number of plots, carving up serpentine paths around which they planted their gardens. They also embedded remnants of scrolls and cornices from the Riverside and Riviera theaters into the flower beds as reminders of the site's history. Three serviceberry trees, weighing five hundred pounds each, came as a donation from Rockefeller Center, where they had been languishing on the roof terrace.

The garden earned its name from the lotus plants that grow in its pair of ponds. As the story goes, back when the garden was being installed, a man who had been growing lotuses in tubs in his living room came by and asked if he could temporarily leave them in the ponds. Since then, various new lotuses have been added, sending up gorgeous blooms in these ponds every summer.

Today thirty gardeners of all ages and experience levels tend these plots. Mature trees,

established 1983 **total acreage** 0.16 **entrance** 250 West 97th Street
public transit 96 St ❶❷❸ **website** thelotusgarden.org

fragrant flowers, and climbing vines greet visitors as they crest the flight of stairs. One garden member wrote a book in the garden over the course of a summer. Another, who is a teacher, grades papers among the flowers. At Halloween, neighborhood children in costumes gather to collect their treats. Kids have grown up in the garden, helping their parents nurture the plants and finding joy in friendship and community.

Novice gardeners learn not only about caring for plants but also about the natural cycle of loss and renewal.

Like the lotus plant itself, which survived the Ice Age and rises out of the muddy water to offer its exquisite flower, the Lotus Garden sprang out of the wreckage of the once-opulent theaters, fueled by the obstinacy of New Yorkers who wanted to garden against all odds.

ABOVE: The garden is an island of greenery and flowers in summer, with hydrangeas under the magnolia tree, *left*, and lilies in the flower bed, *right*. OPPOSITE: A seating area by the ivy-clad wall.

Tudor City Greens

A quiet corner on the edge of Midtown

Even for longtime residents, New York City remains full of beautiful surprises. Tudor City Greens, tucked away at the eastern end of Forty-Second Street, is a historic hideaway that few New Yorkers know about. Composed of two small parks linked by an overpass, this tranquil leafy spot—one of the best secret green spaces in the city—is open to the public every day of the year. For those in the know, Tudor City Greens is Gramercy Park without the key.

Shaded by canopies of mature trees, the parks contain gathering areas with comfortable benches, bistro chairs, and tables set up in different configurations to facilitate meetings, outdoor lunches, or quiet reading time alone. The sunnier South Park has an open layout that invites more congregation, making it the site of concerts and events. In the North Park, the tall trees and surrounding buildings create a more secluded and contemplative environment. Flowers bloom throughout the seasons in both parks while the skyscrapers of Midtown are banished behind the trees.

Tudor City was the project of real estate developer Fred F. French, who built the residential development in the late 1920s on the escarpment overlooking First Avenue, between East Forty-First and Forty-Third Streets. Designed to provide all the amenities of suburban living while being centrally located in town, Tudor City is anchored by its parks. Eschewing the courtyard gardens that were popular in grand buildings at the time, the developer placed Tudor City Greens outside, making them the focus of the apartment buildings. At the time, the East River was an industrial area of slaughterhouses, meatpacking

facilities, and the coal-burning Con Edison plant. The original gardens, with arbors and fountains, gazebos and shady paths, provided a welcome relief from the pollution and hubbub along the river. There was even an eighteen-hole miniature golf course so residents could unwind in the evening and on weekends.

Like many gardens in the city at one time or another, Tudor City Greens was threatened with bulldozers when the development was sold to Helmsley Spear, whose plans to replace the open spaces with high-rise towers were stopped by neighborhood residents who formed a human chain around the parks. Recognizing the importance of green space to the neighborhood, Tudor City's next owner donated the land to the Trust for Public Land, which protects it from future development.

Today the parks are owned and maintained by a nonprofit organization that keeps them in verdant splendor all year round, hosting summer evening concerts, Christmas caroling, and a Hanukkah Menorah lighting ceremony not just for Tudor City residents but for the public at large.

Next time you find yourself in this part of town—while visiting the United Nations building, say—stop by these landmarked gardens to enjoy a moment of tranquility among the greenery. The bonus is the magnificent view from the overpass, where Forty-Second Street can be seen all the way west, along with the Chrysler Building and Grand Central Terminal. It's also a perfect viewing spot for Manhattanhenge, the twice-yearly event when the setting sun aligns with the city's grid, turning Manhattan's glass and steel canyons aglow in a radiant light.

established 1987   **total acreage** 1   **entrance** 38 Tudor City Place #24
public transit Grand Central–42 St ❹❺❻❼❽, Metro-North trains
website tudorcitygreens.org

Elizabeth Street Garden

An eclectic sculpture garden in Little Italy

With stone sphinxes and lions guarding its entrance, Elizabeth Street Garden is an urban oasis with a character all its own. The sentries are joined by several Greek goddesses, a cherub atop one of the ornate birdbaths, a bronze hound, Roman columns, and a wealth of salvaged architectural elements, all happily ensconced among the trees and flowering shrubs. This enchanting green island in a sea of asphalt is Little Italy's hipster version of Florence's Boboli Gardens.

Wedged in among a medley of tenement buildings, restaurants, and trendy boutiques, the community garden reportedly welcomes one hundred thousand visitors a year. Young couples stroll on the gravel path between elegant limestone balustrades that harken back to the Gilded Age. Workers enjoy their lunch on the benches among the flower beds. Readers shrouded in greenery sit engrossed in their books. Schoolchildren prepare to plant seedlings in the raised beds. Others, in groups large and small, gather under the shade of two mature pear trees, planted by the gallerist Allan Reiver when he made the empty lot into a statuary garden three decades ago.

As he recounted in a *New York Times* article, Reiver looked out at the trash-filled lot across the street from his apartment in 1990 and had a vision. The patch of land had once been part of a school; when the school was replaced with an apartment building in 1981, the unused lot was left vacant. "I thought I could make something beautiful out of it," he said. Having obtained a lease from the city, he cleared the space and planted fruit trees and flowers and grass, creating a gallery garden for his neoclassical sculptures. In 2005, he gave the public access to the garden through his

gallery next door. Over time, it became a beloved community space. His son, Joseph Reiver, is now the executive director of the nonprofit Elizabeth Street Garden organization, and manages the garden with a team of volunteers. He describes it as an outdoor museum with free programs (including yoga and tai chi, movie screenings, live music, and poetry readings) and a place for recreation and gathering. Educational gardening programs are provided for students from the local public schools.

Yet this haven of statues and trees and grass is under threat. Volunteers have been battling the city to halt a housing development on the garden's site since 2013. In a city of nearly nine million people, housing is inevitably a pressing need, but green spaces help both locals and visitors connect with the natural world and find community. In the age of climate change, they also bestow myriad benefits on the urban environment, from mitigating the heat island effect to managing stormwater runoff. But there is no way to fully quantify the magic of the garden. In an affidavit for a lawsuit against the city, Allan Reiver wrote, "Destroying Elizabeth Street Garden would not only be a devastating blow to my vision and almost thirty years of work but would cause irrevocable harm to what is now a transformed and vital community and its residents who rely heavily on its presence and amenities."

In the best-case scenario, the garden will be saved as a conservation land trust, and Joseph Reiver will be able to honor his father's legacy with a sustainable future. In the meantime, Elizabeth Street Garden remains a mecca for those seeking to unwind among classical statues, fruit trees, and fragrant flowers.

established 1990   **total acreage** 1   **entrance** Elizabeth Street between Prince and Spring Streets   **public transit** Spring St **❻** and Broadway-Lafayette St **❽❹❺❻**   **website** elizabethstreetgarden.com

Governors Island

An island of green space, open sky, art, culture, and panoramic views

New York is a city of reinvention. Derelict piers can be reimagined as sports fields, picnic lawns, and flower meadows. Governors Island, once an abandoned former military base, is now a unique green island and a destination for art, cultural performances, and recreation. Since its opening to the public in 2005, the island has become a popular summer getaway, drawing ten thousand visitors a day on a typical weekend. It is now a year-round pastoral retreat, its magnificent beauty just eight hundred yards from the southern tip of Manhattan and even closer from Red Hook.

The original island was much smaller than the one we know today, merely sixty-nine acres of land thick with chestnut, hickory, and oak forests. The native Lenape used it as a seasonal hunting and fishing ground, calling it Paggank, meaning "Nut Island." Dutch settlers translated the name to Noten Eylandt. When the British officially took over in 1699, the colonial governor established a headquarters there, renaming it Governors Island.

For over a century from the late 1700s, the island served at various times as an army outpost, a holding facility for Confederate prisoners, and a garrison. Six generals' houses, now known as Colonels Row, were built in the late 1800s, when a community of officers, enlisted men, and their families made their home on the island. In 1911, 103 acres were added to the southern end using rock and earth excavated in the construction of the subway line on Lexington Avenue. Decades later, the US Coast Guard took over the island, making it the service's largest installation with a residential community of about three thousand. After the Coast Guard moved out in 1996, the island remained for many years a wasteland of deserted military buildings.

In 2001, President Bill Clinton designated the northern twenty-two acres as a national park, including Fort Jay and Castle Williams, to be managed by the National Park Service. The federal government sold the remaining 150 acres of Governors Island to the people of New York for a dollar. Since then, many ideas have been pitched for the use of the island: a casino, a soccer stadium, a free-trade zone, a red-light district, an amusement park, and even a prison to replace Guantánamo.

Today Governors Island is accessible by ferry from both Manhattan and Brooklyn, providing New Yorkers with 172 acres of green space that fully embraces the ecology, history, and culture of its singular location. Old converted barracks house the New York Harbor School, a public high school specializing in maritime studies and part of the Billion Oyster Project, whose goal is to restore oyster reefs to New York Harbor. Aspiring urban farmers can learn about agriculture and green infrastructure at GrowNYC Teaching Garden, an urban farm with a greenhouse, several rainwater harvesting systems, a solar oven, and an outdoor kitchen. At the Lavender Field, the only one in the city, Earth Matter volunteers maintain over five hundred plants of four different varieties to create a fragrant oasis for both park goers and pollinators.

The biggest transformation of the island is the creation of the Hills, part of the eighty-seven-acre public park designed by the Dutch architects West 8. A series of hills rising from twenty-five to seventy feet above sea level lifts most of the island out of the flood zone to ensure its resiliency in the face of climate change while also referencing the

established 2001 **total acreage** 172 **public transit** Soissons Landing **GI** and Yankee Pier **SB** ferry stops **website** govisland.com

hilly landscape of Mannahatta. More than forty thousand shrubs were planted on the hills, many of them chosen to withstand harsh maritime conditions and a warming climate. The nearly three thousand trees planted will turn areas of the island into forests in a few decades, making Governors Island a truly green oasis.

Outlook Hill, the tallest of the four hills, offers a panoramic view of New York Harbor, the Statue of Liberty, and the skylines of Manhattan, Brooklyn, and Jersey City. Granite seawall blocks, originally installed during the island's expansion in 1911, were reclaimed to construct the Scramble, the shortcut leading up to the top. Slide Hill offers a series of slides, the most thrilling of which is a curving fifty-seven-foot-long, three-story-high slide.

On Discovery Hill, standing thirty-nine feet above the sea, is the artist Rachel Whiteread's

ABOVE AND OPPOSITE, *from left to right*: A stately elm tree, one of many on the Parade Ground in front of Colonels Row; Liggett Hall, a Georgian Revival building designed by McKim, Mead & White, was part of the former barracks;

permanent installation *Cabin*, a concrete reverse cast of a wooden shed surrounded by bronze casts of actual detritus found on the island. The work is both an evocation of Thoreau and a response to the island's unique vantage point on New York Harbor and the haunting absence of the Twin Towers on the Manhattan skyline. The power of *Cabin* lies in its site-specific condition, its relationship to the air, sky, and ground beneath it.

The robust program of public art projects has turned the island into a cultural backyard for New York City. Former officers' houses now accommodate artist residencies, exhibitions, and art fairs. Site-specific and immersive art installations and performances engage with the island's history and environmental issues. One of the most popular events is the annual Jazz Age Lawn Party. Every year on a June weekend,

artist Rachel Whiteread's permanent installation *Cabin* on Discovery Hill; with five miles of bike paths, the island is a popular destination for cyclists.

thousands of New Yorkers disembark at Soissons Landing dressed in *Great Gatsby*-period costumes for an afternoon picnic of music, cocktails, croquet, and dancing on Colonels Row.

While just a short ferry ride away, Governors Island is a world apart from the city, with no cars but plenty of green space, open sky, and history. Come to the island to experience art and culture amid an expansive landscape with green lawns, lush gardens, and historic buildings. Climb the hills for the breathtaking views. Chill out in a hammock among the trees. Discover the island on bike. From a summer fishing camp to a prison camp to a military garrison, the island has been through many iterations over the centuries. Currently it is a public park, a welcome oasis that will always retain its magic as an island of peace amid a bustling city, accessible to all New Yorkers.

ABOVE, *left*: Adirondack chairs under the shade of a tree; *right*: A view of the Freedom Tower from Discovery Hill. OPPOSITE: The Statue of Liberty, seen from Picnic Point. FOLLOWING PAGES: The Scramble.

Irish Hunger Memorial

A slice of Ireland in Battery Park City

On the edge of Battery Park City stands New York's most unique green space. Variously described as the city's equivalent of the Vietnam War Memorial in Washington, an urban tumulus (an ancient burial mound), and a sculpture imbued with historical references, the Irish Hunger Memorial is at once an emotionally resonant landscape and a singular work of public art.

The monument, designed by the artist Brian Tolle in collaboration with the landscape architect Gail Wittwer-Laird and the architectural firm 1100 Architect, is a platform cantilevered over a stratified base of glass and fossilized Irish limestone, tilting sharply twenty-five feet aboveground at the entrance. The entrance leads through a passageway lined with some eight thousand linear feet of text projected through thin bands of backlit glass. The mutable text, which includes poems, songs, statistics, testimonials, and quotations, sheds light on the Great Hunger and the ongoing struggle with famine worldwide. Recorded voices amplify the written words' invitation to reflect on past and present trials. At the end of the passageway stands a nineteenth-century cottage, lifted from County Mayo and reconstructed here, stone by stone. Like many cottages from the era whose roofs were torn off as proof of destitution and thus qualification for relief, it remains roofless.

The craggy hillside, planted with flora native to the Connacht wetlands—heaths and heathers, blackthorn and burnet rose, gorse and thistle—is a fragment of Ireland filled with memory of the tragedy. The landscape is strewn with stones inscribed with the names of all the counties of Ireland. The quarter-acre size of the field is a reminder of the Gregory Clause passed by the British Parliament in 1847, which effectively compelled relief applicants to surrender all but a quarter of an acre of their land or die of hunger. A dirt path climbs to the top of the hill, where the vista of the Hudson River, the Statue of Liberty, and Ellis Island recalls the Diaspora, when more than a million Irish sought refuge from the Great Hunger on distant shores. Many landed here in New York and continue to shape the history of this city.

For decades, efforts to build a memorial in New York to Ireland's Great Hunger (*An Gorta Mór* in Gaelic) of 1845 to 1852 led nowhere. It was not until 2000, following a visit to Ireland, that Governor George Pataki and Battery Park City Authority president Timothy S. Carey took concrete steps to realize the project. Vesey Green, blocks away from the Twin Towers, was chosen as the site of the memorial. Construction began in March 2001 and was halted halfway through by the 9/11 attack. The Irish Hunger Memorial opened to the public in July 2002 in the heart of a downtown New York still deep in grief.

The memorial is a contemplative space where the story of a bitter famine is meaningfully told in the landscape. As the writer Simon Schama wrote in the *New Yorker*, "the experience of the place . . . doubles in significance: both trauma and hope, departure and arrival, exile and rescue." It may be experienced as a living sculpture, a green space, and a compelling monument, but most of all, it is an extraordinary public memorial that offers a journey into the past and demands a response to current world events.

established 2002   **total acreage** 0.5   **entrance** 290 Vesey Street   **public transit** Chambers St ❶❷❸ and World Trade Center ❸; Battery Park City/Vesey St ferry stop **SG**

The High Line

Flower meadows, woodland, and prairie grasses reclaim an abandoned railway

The origin story of the High Line is a compelling saga of two young New Yorkers who, through imagination and perseverance and determination, redefined what a twenty-first-century park can be.

Beginning in the nineteenth century, the West Side of Lower Manhattan was a busy industrial waterfront. Ships, trains, and trucks ferried agricultural and industrial goods to the warehouses and factories that fringed the area's avenues. Between 1929 and 1934, the High Line—then called the West Side Elevated Line—was built to run two stories aboveground, cutting through some buildings to bring meat, dairy, and produce directly to warehouses. It operated for nearly five decades, until the last freight train delivered three carloads of frozen turkey to their destination on Gansevoort Street in 1980. Then it sat empty for some twenty years, as grasses, wildflowers, shrubs, and trees took root between the train tracks, returning an industrial landscape back to arcadia.

What some saw as a fascinating vestige of New York's industrial and transportation history worth saving, others saw as an unsightly relic to be torn down. In the latter camp were developers who clamored to have it demolished, pointing out a litany of complaints against the defunct railway—that it was an eyesore, a danger, and a blight to the neighborhood. In 1999, Joshua David, a travel writer, and Robert Hammond, an entrepreneur and part-time painter, founded Friends of the High Line to advocate for its preservation and readaptation as a park in the sky. What David and Hammond found on the abandoned railway was a wild landscape of unusual beauty, perched above the city streets and surrounded by its landmarks, a treasure hidden in plain sight. As Hammond recalled in the book *High Line: The Inside Story of New York City's Park in the Sky*, "It was another world, right in the middle of Manhattan."

From April 2000 to July 2001, Hammond and David engaged photographer Joel Sternfeld to document the High Line through all seasons, and the resulting images would come to define the project and propel it forward. Sternfeld's evocative photographs were accompanied by the words of the *New Yorker* writer Adam Gopnik, who painted an idyllic picture of the derelict train track overtaken by "irises and lamb's ears and thistle-tufted onion grass, white-flowering bushes and pink-budded trees and grape hyacinths, and strange New York weeds that shoot up with horizontal arms, as though electrified." Added to this, a flock of warblers, a stand of hardwood trees, and "an almost Zen quality of measured, peaceful distance."

The essential design challenge of the project became finding the balance between preserving the magic of the existing wild landscape generated by years of abandonment and adapting it for a park to be used by millions of people. In 2003, Friends of the High Line held an open ideas competition and received 720 entries from thirty-six countries. One entry proposed turning the railway into a mile-long swimming pool. Another suggested leaving the landscape intact and putting in a roller coaster. Significantly, most of the entries showed a love for the existing landscape. As Robert Hammond recalled, one commenter at the Grand Central exhibition of the

established 2009   total acreage 6.7   entrances 10th Avenue at West 30th Street, West 23rd Street, and West 14th Street   public transit Ⓐ Ⓒ Ⓔ between 14 St & 8 Av and 34 St–Penn Station, ❶ ❷ ❸ between 14 St & 7 Av and 34 St–Penn Station, 14 St–Union Sq & 8 Av Ⓛ, and 34 St–Hudson Yards ❼   website thehighline.org

competition entries wrote: "The High Line should be preserved, untouched, as a wilderness area. No doubt you will ruin it. So it goes."

The job eventually went to a team headed by James Corner Field Operations, Diller Scofidio + Renfro, and Piet Oudolf. To reinvent the rusty elevated railroad as a public park, it was necessary to dismantle it. Old lead paint had to be removed, concrete repaired, and waterproof work completed before the whole thing was put back together again, section by section. To preserve the vision of nature reclaiming its place, the architects essentially designed the park as a long path meandering through varied conditions—woodland giving way to grassland, wildflower meadow to lawn, wetland to thicket. Trees rise out of railway tracks, and walkways dissolve into flower beds. The Dutch plantsman

ABOVE AND OPPOSITE: Inspired by the wild landscape that grew on the railway line when it was abandoned for twenty-five years, the planting design of the High Line is a rich tapestry of trees, grasses, and perennials. On the

Piet Oudolf, known for a measure of wildness in his planting compositions, chose hundreds of species of grasses, wildflowers, shrubs, and trees for the High Line. Many are natives, some are derived from the original self-sown landscape, all are drought tolerant. They form a ribbon of green weaving their way through twenty-two blocks, floating between buildings from the Meatpacking District to Midtown, shifting and changing through the year: exuberant with flowers in the warm seasons and stripped down to sculptural forms and textures in the cold months.

Ten years after the founding of the Friends of the High Line, and despite a demolition order that Mayor Rudy Giuliani signed during his last days in office, the first section of the High Line, from Gansevoort to Twentieth Street, opened to the public in 2009. The mystery and

Washington Grasslands and Woodland Edge, tall grass and bare trees form a composition in gold in winter, while blooming dogwood and redbud herald spring in April.

haunting atmosphere captured by Joel Sternfeld's photographs and Adam Gopnik's prose are inevitably lost, but the park gave New Yorkers a new perspective of the city—from thirty feet above street level—and redefined the urban experience of nature.

While the architects' details, such as the linear concrete planks that rise up in places to become benches, the capacious wooden deck chairs rolling along the track north of Pier 54, and the amphitheater overlooking Tenth Avenue, are highly innovative, the stars of the park are the plants. Tall prairie grasses bask in the sun, waving in the wind. Drifts of flowers—purple coneflowers, black-eyed Susans, astilbes, northern blazing stars, yarrows, foxtail lilies, Queen Anne's lace, wild bergamots—meld into one another, their bright colors in summer deepening into a

ABOVE AND OPPOSITE: One of the reasons for the High Line's success is its ability to redefine the urban experience through an exuberant injection of nature. *From left to right*: A floriferous elderflower shrub; thistle-like flowers of

palette of burnished golds, dark reds, and tawny browns in fall. A flyover rising eight feet above the railway between Twenty-Fifth and Twenty-Seventh Streets offers a walk amid the canopy of magnolia, sassafras, and serviceberry trees. On the sundeck, native sumac trees cut their graceful silhouettes against the gleaming Hudson River. Nature, rising against the cityscape, is insistent in all its lyrical beauty, through all seasons.

The 1.45-mile park was completed in 2019, with the opening of its northern end, the Spur, on Thirtieth Street and Tenth Avenue. Its success has radically altered the neighborhood with the proliferation of luxury residential buildings, but New York is a place of constant change. The High Line, through its evolution from decay to rebirth, bridges the city's industrial past and high-tech future with its celebration of nature.

rattlesnake master; smoke bush and purple coneflower; hardy hibiscus. FOLLOWING PAGES, *left*: Dogwoods blooming between railway tracks; *right*: Drifts of flowers in summer. PAGES 130–131: The Diller-von Furstenberg Sundeck.

Franklin D. Roosevelt Four Freedoms State Park

A meditative space at once removed from and a part of the city

Lying between Manhattan and Queens, Roosevelt Island is a quiet residential community with the charm of a small town. In the month of April, the promenade with its canopy of cherry blossoms and striking views of the city makes the island a popular destination. But what draws tourists from all over the world to Roosevelt Island is the Franklin D. Roosevelt Four Freedoms State Park.

One of New York City's architectural treasures, the park lies at the southernmost tip of the island, framed by Manhattan to the west and Queens to the east. The last monument designed by Louis I. Kahn, the memorial to Roosevelt is a beautiful landmark in its elegant geometry and unadorned materials—trees, granite, paving. Though not a typical park (no picnicking on the lawn), the memorial offers a contemplative space like none other in the city. It is, as the architect's daughter Sue Ann Kahn describes it, "a work of great power and clarity."

In 1972, an ambitious plan was hatched to transform what was then known as Welfare Island (which had housed at various points in time a prison, a workhouse, an asylum, and several hospitals) into a residential community. The island would be renamed in Roosevelt's honor, and Mayor John Lindsay advocated a memorial to the former president that "would face the sea he loved, the Atlantic he bridged, the Europe he helped to save, the United Nations he inspired." Kahn was commissioned to design the monument, which he completed before his death in 1974. However, it would take nearly four decades to bring it to fruition.

The architect based his design on the simple concept of "a room and a garden," with echoes of a classical Greek temple. At the park's entrance, a row of copper beech trees stands as a welcoming prelude to the monument. On the other side of the trees, a climb to the top of the ceremonial staircase reveals a grand vista of the garden. Two allées of little-leaf linden trees flanking a triangular lawn converge upon a colossal bust of Roosevelt, held aloft in a spacious granite box. The narrowing garden, its pristine grass and uniformly shaped trees framing the panorama of the cityscape over the East River, gently slopes downward toward the tip of the island, culminating at the "room," a plaza with three walls made of granite blocks spaced an inch apart, their sides polished to reflect light and amplify narrow views of Manhattan and Queens. Inscribed on the back of the granite holding Roosevelt's bust are words from his "Four Freedoms" speech, delivered in 1941, in which he defined the universal freedoms of speech and expression, of worship, from want, and from fear. This roofless room is the symbolic heart of the memorial, a contemplative space under an open sky. The vista over the stirring waters of the East River toward the Atlantic and beyond reinforces Roosevelt's hopeful words on his vision for the world.

Kahn's only work in New York City is a monument of light, space, and silence. As the *New York Times* architecture critic Michael Kimmelman wrote upon its opening, the monument "gives New York nothing less than a new spiritual heart."

---

established 2012 **total acreage** 4 **public transit** Roosevelt Island **Ⓕ**; Roosevelt Island tram; Roosevelt Island ferry stop **AST** **website** fdrfourfreedomspark.org

Pier 26

A waterfront park for exploring the city's marine wildlife and habitats

The revitalized Pier 26 in the Hudson River Park is part of a new wave of ecological waterfront parks to reclaim New York City's connection to its surrounding rivers. Opened to the public in October 2020, the ecologically themed park focuses on the ecosystems on the coastline of New York before European settlement.

A sequence of ecological habitats is choreographed to make the visitor's journey from the bulkhead city edge out to the river interesting. It begins with a woodland forest, which can be experienced on an elevated walkway through the trees or on a gravel path at ground level. The landscape shifts along the length of the eight-hundred-foot pier, the trees and ferns of the woodland giving way to an open area of coastal grassland that evokes what the shoreline once looked like. Closer to the river is the maritime scrub, where prickly pear cacti, pines, and beach plums form the first line of defense against rising tides and coastal flooding. The journey culminates at the western edge of the pier with the defining feature of the park, the Tide Deck, a man-made rocky tidal marsh, created with smooth cordgrass and thousands of granite boulders to break the waves and provide shelter for waterfowl. The boulders were selected from upstate and placed one by one into the water, simulating rocky conditions normally found closer to the river's edge. Tidal pools for marine creatures were carved into the rocks. An elevated deck wraps around the marshland in an inverted V, ending in a large platform high over the Hudson. The flooding and ebbing of the river can be observed from the deck twice a day. A lower deck is reserved for tour groups and schoolchildren who want to descend into the marsh to study the Hudson estuary at low tide. In this way, the park doubles as a living laboratory in which to study the seventy species of sea life—including tiny seahorses, flounders, and sea robins, as well as colorful sponges, anemones, and hydroids (small invertebrates related to jellyfish)—that inhabit the estuary.

On the recreational side, Pier 26 offers a sunning lawn, a sports court, deck chairs, and stadium-style bleachers. Two modern gazebos set amid the plantings of the dune scrub are each equipped with a pair of swings. A wall on the north side of the pier has windows opening to the river, barstools, and a counter for coffee cups or laptops.

Pier 26 is a much welcome addition to the Hudson River Park, which runs along more than four miles of waterfront on the west side of downtown Manhattan. In an effort to revitalize New York's crumbling piers and protect maritime wildlife, the Hudson River Park Act of 1998 designated 150 acres of land as well as 400 acres of water as a new park and the only estuarine sanctuary in New York State. In 2015, community members submitted a wish list for what was then a two-and-a-half-acre blank concrete slate on Pier 26. Some wanted space for sports. Others suggested a refuge of quiet and nature. Many saw an opportunity for children to study and connect with the riverine habitats. Pier 26 delivered something for everyone in a landscape that speaks to the ecology of the Hudson River estuary.

established 2020 **total acreage** 2.5 **entrance** Hudson River Greenway between North Moore and Hubert Streets **public transit** Franklin St ❶; Battery Park City/Vesey St ferry stop **SG** **website** hudsonriverpark.org

The gazebo in the maritime scrub

The coastal grassland
OPPOSITE: The woodland

Little Island

A whimsical island on the Hudson River

In May 2021, a year into the pandemic that had all New Yorkers appreciating every bit of green space in the city, the highly anticipated Little Island opened to an eager public. A gift from the mogul Barry Diller and his wife, Diane von Furstenberg, the park is a floating jewel box that took four years to plan and three years to build. As Diller explained, his vision was to create "something for the people of New York, and for anyone who visited—a space that on first sight was dazzling, and upon use made people happy."

The 2.4-acre park, a collaboration between the architectural studio of Thomas Heatherwick, the landscape architect Signe Nielsen, and the engineering firm Arup, sits on 132 concrete "tulip" pods rising out of the Hudson River. The "tulips," each with its own unique shape and profile, make up the undulating topography of the park, disguising its perfect square shape with steep hills that afford elevated vantage points and give the park much-needed additional surface space. For the horticulturally minded, Little Island is a maritime botanic garden that doubles as a playground.

Full of unexpected corners, hills, and overlooks, the park is divided into four quadrants, each one a distinct microclimate—from coastal bluff to woodland and from rolling grassland to an evergreen pinetum. Over a hundred trees were planted, some large enough to give the illusion that the park has been there for years. The dawn redwoods will one day stand over sixty feet tall. Meanwhile, more than three hundred species of shrubs, grasses, perennials, and vines and thousands of bulbs keep the park lush all year round.

Designed to dazzle and to delight, Little Island certainly has New Yorkers enthralled. Along with its luxuriant and colorful plantings, the park holds two amphitheaters, three overlooks, a sloping lawn for picnics, fully accessible winding paths, rock scrambles, and a plaza that doubles as a café and an evening performance space. The sunset views are unbeatable, especially from the Southwest Overlook, which rises sixty-three feet over the Hudson River. Afternoon shows and late-night acts—from storytelling and dance performances to poetry readings and concerts—bring live entertainment for audiences of all ages.

Viewed from certain vantage points, Little Island brings to mind the Hanging Garden of Babylon, or Bruegel's painting of the Tower of Babel, with its multilevel gardens. The floating island is a garden folly disguised as a public park, drawing New Yorkers onto the Hudson River over the remnants of the historic Pier 54. Before its destruction by Superstorm Sandy, the pier served as the point of departure and return for the British Cunard–White Star line in the early twentieth century, then as a gathering place for the West Village's LGBTQ+ community and home of the annual Dance on the Pier event, part of the Pride festivities.

Today, crossing over the old Cunard–White Star line archway at Pier 54—where survivors of the *Titanic* landed back in 1912—park visitors leave behind one island for another, or as Diller likes to think, they leave the city to enter the land of Oz, "an oasis of everything fun, whimsical, and playful."

established 2021 **total acreage** 2.4 **entrance** Pier 55, Hudson River Greenway between West 13th and 14th Streets **public transit** 14 St & 8 Av Ⓐ Ⓒ Ⓔ Ⓛ **website** littleisland.org

A summer evening at the park

Asters and anemones
in bloom in fall

Staten Island

Alice Austen House and Garden

A quiet corner of a bygone New York

Staten Island, easily accessible from Manhattan by a scenic ride on the Staten Island Ferry, is New York's greenest borough. It is home to the city's second largest park, the Staten Island Greenbelt, a series of contiguous tracts of land endowed with mature stands of forest, wetlands, lakes, ponds, and streams. It boasts the first wildlife refuge founded in New York City, the William T. Davis Wildlife Refuge, as well as hiking trails, picnic areas, a golf course, tennis courts, and much more.

The island also hosts what will be the largest park developed in New York City in over a century, Freshkills Park. In one of the most ambitious ecological restoration projects, what was once the world's largest landfill will be transformed into a sustainable park with twenty-two hundred acres of open grasslands, wetlands, meadows, and waterways. The master plan envisions miles of walking, biking, and equestrian paths; fishing piers; promenades; floating gardens; sports fields; and an earthwork monument in remembrance of the September 11 recovery effort that turned Freshkills into a forensic site for Ground Zero debris.

On a much more intimate scale is Alice Austen Park, the site of a historic cottage and garden on the shore of the Narrows in New York Harbor. Built in 1690, the original one-room Dutch farmhouse was transformed in the mid-1800s into a Gothic Revival home named Clear Comfort. For seventy-five years it served as the family home of Alice Austen, a pioneering female photographer (and the first woman on Staten Island to own a car). Her work offers a glimpse into different aspects of New York City during

her lifetime, from the immigrant quarantine stations of the 1890s to the private world of her family and friends, many of whom were rebels like herself. Austen and her friend Maria E. Ward founded the Staten Island Bicycle Club in 1895, and the two collaborated on a book titled *Bicycling for Ladies*. The intrepid photographer's partner of fifty-three years was Gertrude Tate, a schoolteacher and dancer. The couple spent thirty years at Clear Comfort before Austen lost her fortune in the stock market crash of 1929 and was evicted in 1945. Tate and Austen were forced to separate, and for a brief time, Austen lived at New York City's Farm Colony, a poorhouse on Staten Island. She passed away in 1952, and a decade later, Clear Comfort was saved from demolition by a group of historic preservationists that included the photographer Berenice Abbott and the architect Philip Johnson.

In 2017, the Alice Austen House Museum was designated a national site of LGBT history, in addition to being a national landmark. The museum hosts a permanent exhibition celebrating Austen's legacy as well as contemporary shows exploring themes in art and journalistic photography. Take a detour from bustling Manhattan and walk among the tall trees and flower beds in the garden to experience a bygone New York. The house's porch, draped in green vines, remains much as it was when Austen's family gathered in its shade for tea in the afternoon, watching the ships pass by in the harbor. With its sweeping views of Brooklyn and Lower Manhattan, the garden is a serene place to contemplate the wondrous city and its colorful past.

established 1975   **total acreage** 1   **entrances** Edgewater Street, Hylan Boulevard, Abbott St
public transit St George ferry stop **SG**, then **S51** bus to Bay St/Hylan Boulevard
website nycgovparks.org/parks/alice-austen-house-and-park

New York Chinese Scholar's Garden

A garden of poetic pleasure

One of Staten Island's biggest cultural attractions is the Snug Harbor Cultural Center and Botanical Garden, which spans eighty-three acres and was for a century a home for retired sailors. Today there are majestic Greek Revival buildings, New York City's first landmark structures; the Healing Garden, a memorial garden for the Staten Islanders who perished on September 11; a Tuscan garden modeled after Villa Gamberaia in Florence; an English white garden; a rose garden; and a farm. An area that once housed a power plant is now a wetland teeming with plant and animal life. The most remarkable, however, is the New York Chinese Scholar's Garden. Inspired by scholar's gardens from the Ming dynasty (1368–1644), it is one of two authentic classical Chinese gardens in the United States. Steeped in tranquility, traditional scholar's gardens were places in which to paint, write poetry, compose music, or simply contemplate. At the New York Chinese Scholar's Garden, visitors get a glimpse into the world of harmony and beauty sought by Confucians, Taoists, scholars, and monks for centuries.

A winding path through a tall bamboo grove offers a time of meditation before entering the garden itself, which unfolds in a series of exquisitely composed vignettes, like a scroll of landscape paintings. Eight pavilions—connected by long corridors, bridges, and covered walkways—encircle a central courtyard with a large koi pond. Zigzags on the paths and bridges offer shifting perspectives. Views of rocks, water, trees, and blossoms are framed through windows and a moon gate along the way. Each tree and shrub has been carefully selected for shape, color, fragrance, and symbolic

meaning. Pine, plum, and bamboo are the "Three Friends of Winter," embodying the Confucian virtues of endurance, modesty, and fortitude. The garden is a spiritual interpretation of nature, with all the elements of the natural landscape—mountains, rivers, lakes, trees, alleys, hills—assembled to create infinite space within the enclosure.

The brainchild of Frances Paulo Huber, president of the Staten Island Botanical Garden in the 1980s (before it merged with Snug Harbor in 2008), this botanical retreat was conceived to highlight China's contribution to the history of gardens and to connect with the heritage of Snug Harbor's sailors who had been engaged in the China Sea trade. The design came from Zou Gongwu, a scholar of classical Chinese gardens. A team of forty Chinese artists and craftspeople in Suzhou, China's famed garden city, spent a year creating roofs, tiles, bridges, windows, and other architectural elements. Rocks were collected from the rivers of Suzhou for the paths. A fifteen-foot tall *gongshi*, or scholar rock—a representation of mountainous landscapes—was harvested from China's Lake Tai. Using a mortise-and-tenon system of traditional Chinese construction rather than nails and glue, the team assembled on-site in six months all the components of the garden, including the building that seems to float in a lake.

The New York Chinese Scholar's Garden is undoubtedly the hidden gem at the Snug Harbor Cultural Center and Botanical Garden. "The Garden of Poetic Pleasure" reads a plaque at the entrance, in Chinese calligraphy. This portal to a world of poetry and another way of seeing is just a short ferry ride away.

---

established 1999   **total acreage** 1   **entrance** 1000 Richmond Terrace   **public transit** St George ferry stop **SG**, then **S40** bus to Richmond Ter/Sailors Snug Harbor Gate or **S44** to Lafayette Av/ Fillmore St   **website** snug-harbor.org/botanical-garden/new-york-chinese-scholars-garden

Brooklyn

Green-Wood Cemetery

An arboretum, bird-watcher's paradise, and art space in a nineteenth-century cemetery

Before Central Park's creation in 1858, New Yorkers looking to escape the city for a respite amid pastoral scenery flocked to Green-Wood Cemetery, making it for a time a tourist attraction second only to Niagara Falls. Part of the rural cemetery movement that started in 1831 with the founding of Mount Auburn Cemetery near Boston, New York's new burial ground, founded in 1838, was designed as a lush and picturesque park in the English landscape garden style, offering an idealized version of nature that starkly contrasted with the industrialized, bustling metropolis that New York had become. Today the cemetery remains one of the city's most beautiful urban oases while also serving as a repository of history, a world-class arboretum, and an essential part of the green corridor that sustains migrating wildlife in the Northeast.

In colonial New York, burials were restricted to church graveyards or, for the less fortunate, potter's fields. As the population grew in the nineteenth century, health and space concerns led to a movement to create large burial grounds in easily accessible rural areas. Green-Wood was the brainchild of Henry Evelyn Pierrepont, known for his prominent role in the planning of Brooklyn. Together with the military engineer David Bates Douglass, hired to design the cemetery's grounds, Pierrepont found the ideal location upon a terminal moraine with glacial ponds, hidden valleys, rocky outcroppings, and the natural highest point of Brooklyn, rising 216 feet above sea level. Straddling the "Brownstone Brooklyn" neighborhoods to the west and mostly farmland to the east, much of the ground was occupied by an old forest of native growth that suggested the cemetery's name,

Green-Wood. Carving winding paths and roads into the hills and taking advantage of the site's varied topography, Douglass created a naturalistic park with shady groves and wide clearings with dramatic views of the city across the East River. As he described it, Green-Wood was "shade, ruralness, natural beauty, everything, in short, in contrast with the glare, set form, fixed rule, and fashion of the city." To complement Douglass's romantic landscape, the architect Richard Upjohn added the soaring Gothic Revival gates in 1863. Today the many eaves, nooks, and crannies of the archway are home to a flock of monk parrots, immigrants from Argentina that, according to one theory, escaped from JFK Airport in 1967.

The Greek roots of the word *cemetery* mean "a sleeping place." Green-Wood Cemetery reflects the nineteenth century's more serene attitude toward death. Far from the somber graveyards of old, Green-Wood was designed as a place of beauty and a peaceful sanctuary where families could come for Sunday picnics and long walks amid pastoral splendor. Expanded greatly since its founding, the cemetery today encompasses 478 acres, five lakes, groves of majestic trees upon hills and ridges, incomparable vistas, and what the architecture critic Paul Goldberger called "an almost magical kingdom of Greek temples, Renaissance palaces, Egyptian temples, Corinthian columns, obelisks and Gothic towers."

As the final resting place of nearly six hundred thousand New Yorkers, Green-Wood also preserves the rich and diverse history of the city. In residence are more than a few artists and musicians: Jean-Michel Basquiat; Leon Golub

---

established 1838   **total acreage** 478   **entrances** Fifth Avenue and 25th Street; Fourth Avenue and 35th Street; Fort Hamilton Parkway and Micieli Place; and Ninth Avenue and 20th Street
public transit 36 St **ⓓⓝⓡ**, 9 Av **ⓓ**, and Church Av **ⓕⓖ**   **website** green-wood.com

and his wife, Nancy Spero; Leonard Bernstein; Paul Jabara (who wrote Donna Summer's hit "Last Dance" and the Weather Girls' "It's Raining Men"); French-born Camilla Urso (the first woman concert violinist in the United States). Other pioneers interred at Green-Wood include Susan Smith McKinney-Steward, the first Black woman doctor in New York State and the third in the country; Sarah J. Smith Tompkins Garnet, the first

Black principal in the city's public school system; and Violet Oakley, the first woman to receive a public mural commission in the United States. This being New York, there are also eccentrics, like Lola Montez, the dancer who conquered the hearts of King Ludwig I of Bavaria, Czar Nicholas I, and the French writers Honoré de Balzac and Alexandre Dumas before devoting her last years to helping "outcast women."

ABOVE AND OPPOSITE, *from left to right:* Among the nearly seven thousand trees at Green-Wood are giant native tulip trees, the largest of which is over a hundred feet tall and has a trunk nearly six feet in diameter; clusters of white

Beyond its permanent residents, Green-Wood's living treasures are the eight thousand trees and shrubs that contribute to its status as an arboretum. Among the giants are majestic tulip trees. A sassafras specimen is the oldest and largest of the species in all of New York State. The Franklin tree, named after Benjamin Franklin and extinct in the wild since the nineteenth century, is represented here by several examples descended from seeds collected by John Bartram in 1765. Superstorm Sandy in 2012 had a devastating effect on this living collection, taking down three hundred trees, some over 150 years old. The storm prompted a new outlook on Green-Wood's most important natural resources, its plant life. More than three thousand trees have been planted since Sandy's destruction, with species more adapted to the changing climate.

mountain laurel blooming in May; beech, maple, and oak trees line the paths around the cemetery; a blooming fringe tree carpets the ground with its fallen petals.

In parts of the cemetery, lawns have also been converted into meadows.

Green-Wood's verdant landscape is part of a green corridor in Brooklyn that sustains bird migrations through the Atlantic Flyway, making it a bird-watcher's paradise. Herons, egrets, hawks, warblers, terns, finches, and many others can be seen here.

The cemetery also plays host to a robust program of art exhibitions, concerts, and dance performances throughout the year.

With art, history, and nature at its heart, Green-Wood Cemetery is a unique green space in New York City. Come walk these grounds to contemplate the graceful trees, the timeworn monuments, and the stories of bygone New Yorkers.

ABOVE, *left*: The Valentine Angel in bronze; *right*: A more somber angel in stone. OPPOSITE: On Battle Hill, a statue of Minerva with her hand raised toward Lady Liberty.

Prospect Park

Brooklyn's landscape masterpiece by Olmsted and Vaux

Until 1898, when it became a borough of New York City, the independent City of Brooklyn was a thriving metropolis with the third largest population in the country. When Central Park opened in 1858, the citizens of Brooklyn clamored for a sizable park of their own. In the end, Brooklynites got their wish with Prospect Park, designed by the duo who created Central Park, Frederick Law Olmsted and Calvert Vaux. More than a century later, it remains "the foremost art monument of Brooklyn," designed for, approved by, and belonging to the people of this city, as Clay Lancaster, an architecture writer and the park's curator in the 1960s, noted in his *Prospect Park Handbook*.

In 1866, the designers presented their plan, accompanied by a long essay meditating on the purposes of city parks in general and the aesthetics behind their design. The plan was printed and distributed to the citizens of Brooklyn, who gave it "a hearty approval." Construction began the same year and would continue for seven years until its completion in 1873.

The land on Prospect Park offered Vaux and Olmsted the ideal conditions for their pastoral vision. About seventeen thousand years ago, the receding Wisconsinan glacier left a string of gentle hills and kettles in the northern part of the park and an outwash plain in the south. In the nineteenth century, most of the old forest had been cleared for open pasture after two hundred years of European colonialization, but large stands of chestnut, oak, American elm, and tulip trees remained scattered around the site.

Drawing on the "three grand elements of pastoral landscape"—namely verdant meadow, wooded hills, and ample water—the designers composed three distinct regions, all harmoniously woven together by an intricate network of walks, drives, and rambles, some of which retraced ancient trails made by the Indigenous peoples. From the main entrance on the narrow point of Grand Army Plaza, the park unfolds into its three parts. First, the Long Meadow, stretching over ninety acres, was shaped out of hilly pasture and peat bogs. Olmsted planted and moved mature trees with specially designed horse-drawn "tree-moving machines"—wooden wagons with wheels as tall as a man—to be placed singly or in groups over the undulating turf. Trees were in fact the main focus of the designers as the park took form in the beginning. Adding to the native ash, red mulberry, wild cherry, dogwood, sassafras, and Osage orange were thousands of European and Asian trees. English oak, Scotch elm, horse chestnut, and Austrian pine were introduced, along with Chinese elm, the pagoda tree, umbrella pine, magnolia, and others. Some, like the Camperdown elm, came as gifts. Today the Long Meadow is the most popular part of the park, a gathering place for Brooklynites and their canine best friends in the early morning and a sunning and picnicking locale for the rest of the day. After a snowstorm, the meadow is transformed into a winter scene from a Brueghel painting, children sledding down the hills and adults cross-country skiing.

Conceived as the heart of Prospect Park, the Ravine was inspired by the landscape of the Adirondack Mountains. Incorporating the last remnants of the old forest, this central area is home to 150 acres of woodland and waterways.

established 1867 **total acreage** 526 **entrances** Along Prospect Park West, Prospect Park Southwest, Flatbush Avenue, Ocean Avenue, and Parkside Avenue **public transit** Parkside Av and Prospect Pk **B** **Q**, 15 St–Prospect Pk **F** **G**, Grand Army Plaza **2** **3**, and Prospect Park **S** **website** prospectpark.org

165

From the rolling expanse of the Long Meadow, meandering paths take park goers through shady groves of towering trees, babbling streams, and steep gorges. This woodland is Brooklyn's only forest, thick with everything from oaks to black birch to hickory, and rich in wildlife, from woodpeckers and hawks to mallards and herons.

Winding its way through the Ravine is an intricate watercourse—the third grand element in the park's design—that starts at the top of Fallkill Falls, cascades under the Binnen Bridge, and pours into the vast fifty-five-acre lake at the south end of the park. Along the way, the water gathers in various narrow lagoons, pools, and waterfalls, creating rich habitats for water's edge flora and fauna. The lake is one of Brooklyn's most popular spots for catch-and-release fishing, boasting the largest population of largemouth bass in the state.

ABOVE: Prospect Park Lake, seen here on a fall morning, is one of the three essential elements of the pastoral landscape that Frederick Law Olmsted and Calvert Vaux created at Prospect Park.

Opened in 1867 while still incomplete, the park was an immediate success. Picnicking, while prohibited at Central Park at the time, became hugely popular at Prospect Park, such that the twelve hundred picnic tables provided in the 1920s were barely enough to accommodate demand. In the century-plus since Vaux and Olmsted completed their work, the park has undergone periods of change, decline, and rebirth. The early 1900s saw several neoclassical additions to its grounds, including the transformation of the main entrances and the construction of the Peristyle (in 1904), the Boathouse (in 1905), and the Tennis House (in 1910). Robert Moses, New York City's parks commissioner for twenty-six years, singlehandedly had the most impact on Vaux and Olmsted's work. His many projects

ABOVE: The Long Meadow, stretching over ninety acres, is popular with picnickers, flaneurs, and dog owners.
FOLLOWING PAGES: A winter scene on the Long Meadow.

over three decades, including the zoo, the bandshell, playgrounds, and a skating rink and accompanying two-hundred-car parking area, led to the destruction of many of the nineteenth-century structures. The city's proposed demolition of the Boathouse in 1964 prompted the creation of a preservation group, the Friends of Prospect Park, to ensure the conservation of historical structures and endangered flora within the park.

Today the ongoing recovery and maintenance of the park is carried out by the Prospect Park Alliance, a nonprofit organization founded in 1987. The alliance's most ambitious project is the LeFrak Center at Lakeside, which replaced the Moses-era Wollman Rink with a year-round recreational facility and restored Music Island and the Esplanade to Vaux and Olmsted's original design. The 1905 Boathouse is now the nation's

ABOVE AND OPPOSITE: Trees were the focus of Olmsted and Vaux early in their planning, and today there are more than 175 species in the park. *From left to right*: Saucer magnolias, with their spectacular bloom in spring, are some of

first urban Audubon Center, taking advantage of the diverse wildlife and habitats created by Vaux and Olmsted. The alliance has also been planting a corridor of native flowers through the park to sustain wildlife.

Prospect Park, as its designers insisted, is a work of art, characterized by its pastoral, picturesque, and sublime aesthetic ideals borrowed from centuries of European landscape paintings.

Olmsted and Vaux's Brooklyn monument is a living work of art created "for all classes of our community, enabling thousands to enjoy pure air, with healthful exercise, at all seasons of the year," as James Stranahan, the head of the Brooklyn Park Commission for twenty-two years and the park's most ardent champion, wrote over 150 years ago. The ten million people who enjoy its grounds every year would heartily agree.

the most beautiful; a grove of Siberian elm near the Dog Beach; a waterfall in the Ravine, Brooklyn's last remaining forest; trees in their winter coats.

Brooklyn Botanic Garden

Inspiring, healing, and illuminating gardens

For over a century, the Brooklyn Botanic Garden has been a valuable resource for the borough's home gardeners, advocating environmental stewardship, fostering sustainable horticultural practices, and inspiring connection with nature through its many beautiful gardens.

Founded in 1910 with botanist Charles Stuart Gager as director, the garden was originally designed by the Olmsted Brothers firm. It opened officially the following year with the Native Flora Garden (called the Local Flora Section at the time) as the first display garden. Over the next century, it would continue to be developed and expanded, with various areas devoted to different specialty gardens, habitats, and taxa of plants.

Completed in 1915, the Japanese Hill-and-Pond Garden was one of the first public Japanese gardens in the country. Working with a limited budget, the designer Takeo Shiota mixed classical elements of a Japanese hill-and-pond garden with his own flourishes. A grand torii gate—a demarcation between a sacred shrine and ordinary space—rising over the water was modeled after the great torii gate of Itsukushima Shrine, which stands in the Seto Inland Sea. With his composition of gentle hills, curving pond, and cascading waterfall constructed from local Manhattan schist by Italian masons, Shiota reimagined the garden as a three-dimensional landscape imbued with symbolic meanings, changing colors with the seasons, evoking both the eternal and the ephemeral. The pines stand tall in permanence while the falling water brings constant change. In spring, weeping cherry trees are the first to bloom, draping over the pond, their various shades of pink reflected in the water. In early May come clusters of pale purple wisteria, made more delicate in contrast to the deep crimson foliage of the Japanese maple trees. Autumn brings a symphony of foliage in bright yellow and ocher to red, violet, and rust. Pale pink camellia blooms envelop the wooden waiting bench. Except for a period during World War II when anti-Japanese sentiment forced its closure and arson gutted the Shinto shrine, the Japanese Hill-and-Pond Garden has remained a favorite destination for New Yorkers and tourists alike who find refuge from the frenzied city in this harmonious and timeless landscape, trading traffic noise for birdsong and the sound of falling water, watching the ducks make their way across the pond while the turtles sun themselves on warm rocks.

Behind the Japanese Hill-and-Pond Garden is the Cherry Walk and Cherry Esplanade, a large lawn bordered by two allées of flowering cherry and red oak trees. The garden's flowering cherry collection includes more than twenty-five species and cultivars, with flowers in every form and shade, from dazzling white to hot pink. *Hanami*, the cherry blossom viewing season, begins with *Prunus × incam* 'Okame' and *P. hirtipes*, whose blossoms come out at the same time as the daffodils. The garden celebrates this season with performances by dancers, taiko drummers, and samurai sword masters, drawing thousands of visitors under the canopy of extravagant hot pink 'Kanzan' cherry blossoms to enjoy their ephemeral beauty.

The Brooklyn Botanic Garden today has expanded to fifty-two acres, with over 14,000 taxa

established 1910   total acreage 52   entrances 150 Eastern Parkway, 455 Flatbush Avenue, and 990 Washington Avenue   public transit Prospect Pk ❷❹, Botanic Garden ❺, and Eastern Pkwy–Brooklyn Museum ❷❸   website bbg.org

of plants, a conservatory with a bonsai collection, an aquatic plant house, three climate-themed plant pavilions, and an array of specialty gardens. The Bluebell Wood is an enchanting destination for a woodland walk in spring when a carpet of Spanish bluebells bursts into bloom under a mature stand of oak, birch, and beech trees.

June is the time to visit the Cranford Rose Garden, where thousands of fragrant blooms—from species and old heritage roses to modern hybrids—fill the formal beds, clamber up pavilions and lattices, and drape over arches and swags. The Discovery Garden, redesigned in 2015, is made especially for young naturalists to explore and learn about plants and animals in different habitats. Both educational *and* beautiful, the herb garden, opened in 2010, features a small orchard and a variety of food and medicinal plants with

ABOVE AND OPPOSITE: The Japanese Hill-and-Pond Garden was one of the first public Japanese gardens in the country. *From left to right*: The viewing pavilion, built in the style of a teahouse; wisterias in bloom; the pond at the

helpful explanation of their origins and uses and practical gardening advice to inspire those making gardens out of backyards, windowsills, and fire escapes.

The new Shelby White and Leon Levy Water Garden, part of the Water Conservation Project and completed in 2016, is a one-and-a-half-acre garden inspired by New York's wetlands. Hardy hibiscus, queen-of-the-prairie, gray goldenrod, great blue lobelia, and New England asters—mixed with ferns, shrubs, and trees—keep the Water Garden vibrant and lush while providing food for wildlife, filtering and recirculating rainwater, and drastically reducing freshwater consumption throughout the gardens. On the new Robert W. Wilson Overlook, built in 2019, a ribbon of native grasses, wild roses, asters, black-eyed Susans, and coneflowers frame a fully accessible zigzagging

center of the garden; the red torii gate glimpsed through the plantings. FOLLOWING PAGES: The Bluebell Wood at its peak, in early May.

path up to the top, where sweeping views of the Cherry Esplanade and the Cranford Rose Garden are on offer. A collection of crape myrtles, a southern plant that has become increasingly common in New York as the climate warms, adds colorful clusters of blooms in late summer and bright red to purple foliage in fall. Water lilies and lotuses put on a brilliant display on the Lily Pool Terrace in July, August, and September.

Since its beginning, the Brooklyn Botanic Garden has been educating New Yorkers on the ecological and cultural importance of gardens, allowing residents to connect with the beauty and healing power of nature. At no time is this more evident than in May, when the tree peony collection explodes into bloom. After the September 11 terrorist attacks, the Japanese town of Yatsuka-Cho made a present of three

ABOVE: Colorful vegetables and herbs (including artichokes, *right*) fill the Herb Garden at harvesttime. OPPOSITE: The fully accessible path on the Robert W. Wilson Overlook winds its way through a landscape of native grasses and

hundred specimens representing forty-nine cultivars of tree peonies to "bring peace of mind to the people of the United States." The shipment was sent in September the following year, but a dockworker lockout in California caused the shipping container to sit on the docks for weeks. All the plants perished. The people of Yatsuka-Cho generously sent another shipment, which arrived safely in early December, during an arctic cold blast. The peonies were planted in the frozen ground during a snowstorm. They survived to be one of the largest collections of tree peonies in the United States, flowering every spring—hundreds of rare blooms, in white, yellow, red, pink, purple, and maroon, all of unparalleled extravagance and beauty. To witness these blooms is to be reminded that beauty will triumph over brutality, care over violence, and friendship over enmity.

perennials, which culminates in a rich composition of textures in late October. FOLLOWING PAGES: The tree peony collection blooming in May.

Gil Hodges Community Garden

A tiny oasis playing a crucial role in the city's green infrastructure

This is no ordinary garden. On a corner lot of just over 3,100 square feet near the Gowanus Canal, Gil Hodges Community Garden might look like the neighborhood's busy backyard, but this sliver of green in the midst of industrial and commercial buildings does double duty as a cog in the city's green infrastructure to protect our waterways.

Major storms like Hurricane Ida in 2021, which unleashed more than three inches of rain in an hour, can overwhelm the sewer system, sending its overflow into the city's waterways. At Gil Hodges Community Garden, stormwater is absorbed, filtered, and diverted to the garden, relieving pressure on the sewer system and thereby protecting the local waterways from contamination.

The Gowanus neighborhood was once a tidal inlet with saltwater marshland teeming with fish and other wildlife. The canal was a meandering creek, its brackish water filled with oyster beds. Dutch settlers named the creek after Chief Gouwane of the local Canarsee nation. On August 27, 1776, American revolutionaries fought a fierce battle against the British along the creek, and many soldiers likely died by drowning in its water. In the mid-nineteenth century, the marshlands were drained and the canal was dug along the two-mile length of the creek. Heavy industries—oil refineries, chemical plants, a cement maker, a soap maker, a tannery, to name a few—sprang up in quick succession, fueling a frenzy that saw as many as seven hundred new buildings constructed in one year. Meadows and marshlands were paved over with concrete and asphalt, making the area flood prone, spilling runoff and contaminated water into the canal, adding to the industrial pollution of the area.

Named after the Brooklyn Dodgers baseball star, Gil Hodges Community Garden had a rather humble beginning; when it first opened in 1982, it was just a large concrete patio, with a smattering of trees and plantings along its perimeter. By 2013, the place needed a major face-lift. Cracks ripped through the patio. The plantings were hardly in better shape. The New York Restoration Project (NYRP), which owns and manages the garden along with fifty-one others in the five boroughs, seized the opportunity to give it a complete makeover, with the added goal of making the small park part of the city's stormwater management system. Funding came from the city's Department of Environmental Protection, which manages New York City's water supply, and Jo Malone London, the British fragrance company.

The foundation underpinning the new garden is a comprehensive system that can absorb 150,000 gallons of stormwater each year. A bioswale—or curbside rain garden—in one of the tree pits, as well as permeable pavers and a rain catchment scheme, diverts the runoff into the garden and out of the stormwater system. Rainwater collected, filtered, and stored in an underground reservoir is used to irrigate the raised beds where local school students grow vegetables and herbs through an after-school program.

To increase biodiversity and promote sustainable horticultural practices, the five tree pits on the sidewalks were enlarged and filled with native plants like winterberry and ironweed. A compost station is installed for use by the maintenance crew, along with neighborhood residents and the church across the street. "Even a local café drops off its food scraps," said Yvi McEvilly, NYRP's director of design.

established 1982   total acreage 0.07   entrance 534 Carroll Street   public transit Union St Ⓡ Ⓦ
website nyrp.org/en/gardens-and-parks/gil-hodges-community-garden

The old concrete patio was broken up and pieces repurposed as stepping-stones in a fragrant walk, where sweet bay magnolia, calycanthus, daphne, and other perfumed flowering shrubs bloom. A pale yellow rosebush near the entrance greets visitors with its heady scented flowers throughout the summer. Long benches, tables, and a blackboard make up an outdoor classroom that also hosts poetry readings, concerts, and art installations. A collaboration with the Brooklyn Academy of Music brought interactive dance performances. The Textile Arts Center down the street has held workshops for the community in the garden. For those in pursuit of quietude and passive recreation, the birch reading grove with cast-stone benches offers a tranquil retreat in the cool shade.

PREVIOUS PAGES: The tiny community garden features raised vegetable beds, a seating area that can function as an outdoor classroom, and a shed with a system to collect rainwater from the roof to use for irrigation.

It will take ten years to remove a century of toxic sludge from the Gowanus Canal. Meanwhile, stormwater management parks like Gil Hodges help keep new pollution from entering the waterway. At the nearby Gowanus Canal Sponge Park on the canal's edge, Susannah C. Drake from DLANDstudio designed what is essentially a wetland with flood-tolerant plantings and a network of sand beds and soils to absorb and filter thousands of gallons of stormwater. As Drake pointed out, her trademark Sponge Park is a working landscape that supports active public engagement with the canal ecosystem. Both parks are models of innovative solutions that make New York City a laboratory for green infrastructure. If one day residents can kayak on the Gowanus Canal—as many dream to—it will be thanks in part to these small but hardworking parks.

OPPOSITE AND ABOVE: Herbs and vegetables grown on the raised beds include, *from left to right*, marigolds, spearmint, kale, and ground-cherries.

Pier 44 Waterfront Garden

An esplanade with spectacular sunset views in Brooklyn's oldest neighborhood

Pier 44 Waterfront Garden, a charming half-mile esplanade on the waterfront between the Atlantic and Erie Basins, reflects both Red Hook's storied past and its vibrant present. Like the Louis Valentino Jr. Park and Pier nearby, it commands expansive views of New York Harbor and the Statue of Liberty—yet many who come here for the views are not aware of the extraordinary history behind this singular corner of New York City.

The Lenape people once enjoyed the marshy coast of Red Hook as a summer site for hunting, fishing, and growing maize and squash in a village called Merechkatvikingh. Dutch settlers arriving in 1636 encountered a familiar landscape of wetlands carved up by a sprawling network of tidal creeks. They named it Roode Hoek—literally Red Point—for the color of the soil and the pointed end of the peninsula. Using their expertise in aquatic technology, the Dutch transformed the low-lying marsh into orchards and farms, dotted with tidal mill ponds. During the Revolutionary War, Fort Defiance was constructed on the highest point of the "hoek," where cannons were fired to hold off British ships while Washington's army escaped to New Jersey.

Red Hook entered the industrial age with the creation of the Atlantic and Erie Basins in the nineteenth century. The marshes were filled in and replaced by piers and docks that spread like tentacles into the harbor, erasing the "hoek" and any trace of the Revolutionary War fortifications. For the next hundred years, Red Hook became one of the busiest commercial ports in the country, with up to twenty-six thousand ships passing through its waterways annually, bringing a diverse population into the area. In the early twentieth century, Black longshoremen who had worked Red Hook's docks since the late 1800s were joined by Irish, German, Norwegian, Italian, and Puerto Rican immigrants in search of work in the thriving port.

Many of the nineteenth-century warehouse brick buildings remain as living testaments to Red Hook's industrial past. With its cobblestone streets and row houses, Red Hook today has the relaxed feel of a small village, its denizens an eclectic mix of longtime residents and artists, young families, and small manufacturers attracted by the area's quiet charm. Pier 44 Waterfront Garden opened to the public in 2004, offering a tidal beach and a boardwalk with a garden designed by Lynden Miller. The long and narrow park is also home to the Waterfront Museum, housed aboard a 1914 all-wood barge along the jetty. A small lawn provides a seating area with a panorama of the harbor and its ceaseless maritime activities. Ferries, barges, tugboats, water taxis, and cruise ships crisscross the water at all hours while the Statue of Liberty stands steadfast with her eyes to the sea. Pier 44, like other places on the Red Hook waterfront, affords the rare frontal view of this icon of freedom in the city.

Local families come to the park to walk their dogs and picnic on the lawn. Children tear through the garden in a whirl of shrieking laughter among the plants. People travel from near and far to watch the spectacular sunsets. Some come for early-morning yoga. Runners flock through the garden path in the month before the New York City marathon. Still others come for the flowers in the lush garden that parallels the boardwalk. Maintained by Sarah Burd-Sharps—whose

established 2004   total acreage 0.57   entrance 258 Conover Street at Pier 44 (the gate is at the end of Conover Street)   public transit Beard St/Van Brunt St **B6** bus; Red Hook ferry stop **SB**

husband, David, runs the Waterfront Museum—with the help of a couple of volunteers, the garden is in bloom from early spring to late fall. The planting was especially selected to tolerate the salty water and high winds. Superstorm Sandy buried the garden under six feet of water but, fortunately, the flood didn't linger long. When the water receded, three pine trees perished, but all the perennials survived.

Resilience is built into this corner of Brooklyn that has been shaped for centuries by the forces of geology and human history. At Pier 44 Waterfront Garden, you can walk among flowers, watch the workings of New York Harbor, and contemplate the rich history of the oldest neighborhood in Brooklyn. And while you're here, be sure to also check out the nearby artist-run Pioneer Works and its garden for the vibrant art scene.

ABOVE, *left*: The plants selected by Lynden Miller for the long and narrow garden are salt and wind tolerant; *right*: Peonies blooming in late May. OPPOSITE: A sunset view.

Brooklyn Bridge Park

A postindustrial waterfront park with the spirit of Walt Whitman

When Brooklyn Bridge Park opened in 2010, after eighteen years of planning and design, it was the first new, major park in the borough in more than a century (since the completion of Prospect Park). The new park gave Brooklyn residents a much-needed addition of green spaces—eighty-five acres along more than a mile of tidal shoreline on the East River, linking up with the Empire Fulton Ferry State Park in the north and ending at Atlantic Avenue. The derelict piers where great ships once docked were transformed into sports fields, ball courts, cookout areas, inventive playgrounds, and sunny lawns embraced by native woodlands, all set against an incomparable panorama: the imposing grandeur of the Brooklyn Bridge to the north, the gleaming steel and glass Manhattan skyline to the west, and the torch-bearing Statue of Liberty facing the sea to the south.

While Central Park offered weary nineteenth-century New Yorkers a bucolic escape from the frenzy of the city, Brooklyn Bridge Park embraces the urban backdrop and lively waterway that Walt Whitman once celebrated in his poem "Crossing Brooklyn Ferry." Nature is an integral part of the twenty-first century city, not an illusion of rural countryside inserted into it. By re-creating natural ecologies and using recycled industrial materials, Michael Van Valkenburgh's design addresses the concern for the environment while redefining the urban landscape itself.

On Pier 1, cascading stairs made from granite salvaged from the old Roosevelt Island Bridge turn into an amphitheater for book readings and performances. Native woodlands, densely planted with oak, sweet gum, and locust trees, will eventually form a large canopy like those that once existed in the region. The rising trees temper the ocean winds and filter the summer sun, offering refuge for park goers and butterflies alike. A series of freshwater gardens whose shady paths are brightened with spring flowers serves double duty as a highly engineered stormwater management system and habitat for native birds, insects, and turtles. These wetlands also boast some of the most spectacular fall colors in the park. In front of Jane's Carousel, rainwater collected in the bioswale is filtered by thousands of flowers before flowing back out to the river. A salt marsh is maintained with smooth cordgrass to replicate a natural habitat for ducks and other waterfowl that once dominated the Northeast coast. Rising out of the remains of a sunken railroad transfer barge is Bird Island, an inaccessible and evolving bird sanctuary planted to encourage the growth of a diverse ecology. Over 120 species of birds have been spotted in the park, including fast-flying peregrine falcons, tiny warblers and wrens, and shorebirds like green herons and double-crested cormorants.

The most spectacular ecological feature of the park—a harmonious marriage of ecology and urban park design—is the Flower Field on the rambling Pier 6. Nestled in the southern end of the park, the half-acre meadow is seemingly untamed yet thoughtfully complex, the painterly planting design's true aim being the support of a mosaic of wildlife. A blue wave of camases and blue flag irises in spring morphs into rivers of pink swamp milkweed from summer to

established 2010   **total acreage** 85   **entrances** Along Furman Street, Bridge Park Drive, and Atlantic Avenue   **public transit** York St **F**, High St **A C**, Clark St **2 3**, and Court St **R**; Brooklyn Bridge Park/Atlantic Avenue ferry stop **SB** and Dumbo/Fulton Ferry ferry stop **SB**, **ER**   **website** brooklynbridgepark.org

autumn, filling the meadow with a rose-colored haze and beckoning monarch butterflies from great distances to their favorite food source. Bumblebees buzz around drunk on the nectar of pink turtlehead flowers. Hummingbirds hover in the air, dipping their long, pointed beaks to feed from rose mallows and cardinal flowers. Small songbirds flock to the meadow to forage for tiny insects that live among the plants. In winter,

mature seed heads are left on the plants for wintering birds. Cutbacks in spring leave plant stems at eighteen inches high to foster stem-nesting pollinators.

For park goers, the wild beauty against the rigid geometry of the city skyline is a dazzling visual feast of shifting colors through the seasons. But more than this, the meadow is alive, humming with activity at any time

PREVIOUS PAGES: Drifts of gold false sunflowers and pink joe-pye weed at the Flower Field, a meadow of native wildflowers, in July. ABOVE: Blooming in fall are turtleheads, *left*, and New York asters, *right*.

of year. The Flower Field can be many things at once – a colorful flower garden, a thriving ecosystem created in a postindustrial landscape, and a picturesque oasis in a busy, bustling park. It's thoughtfully maintained by a dedicated horticultural team to give us the sensual delight in seeing masses of flowers in bloom while reminding us of the urgency to re-create the habitats for wildlife that we have destroyed.

Brooklyn Bridge Park has much to offer the entire family. Come see the Flower Field, play pickleball or roller skate on Pier 3, picnic on the lawn, and watch the sun set over the river against the backdrop of Manhattan. In the words of Walt Whitman, what can ever be more stately and admirable than "mast-hemm'd Manhattan? River and sunset and scallop-edg'd waves of flood-tide?"

ABOVE, *left*: Monarch butterflies visit the meadow in late summer to feed on swamp milkweed on their way to Mexico; *right*: Swamp rose mallow and prairie dock.

Views toward the
Statue of Liberty

Brooklyn Grange

Urban farms in the sky

Despite its reputation as a concrete jungle, New York City has a long history of urban farming. The island of Manhattan was a patchwork of farms and meadows, ponds and marshes before the city's grid was laid down in the early nineteenth century. In 1902, Frances Griscom Parsons opened the first farm garden near the tenements on Manhattan's West Side to teach children how to cultivate vegetables. Soon kids were learning to grow corn, beets, beans, carrots, and lettuce in farm gardens throughout the city, from Thomas Jefferson Park in East Harlem to McCarren Park in Brooklyn. In the 1970s, community gardens sprung up in all the boroughs, turning derelict lots into urban farms. With the increasing popularity of green roofs in the early 2000s, New York farmers began reimagining the city's thousands of open flat roofs as the new frontier for urban farming. As Ben Flanner, who cofounded the Eagle Street Rooftop Farm in Greenpoint with Annie Novak and went on to start Brooklyn Grange, observed, "It was a great opportunity to pioneer a movement."

Founded in 2010, Brooklyn Grange debuted its inaugural farm on top of an old furniture factory in Long Island City. Since then, the farm has expanded to other rooftop locations at the Navy Yard and in Sunset Park; most recently, they opened a rooftop farm and orchard at the Javits Center in Manhattan. It is the largest rooftop farm in New York City, providing the city's restaurants, grocery stores, and community-supported agriculture members with more than a hundred thousand pounds of locally grown organic produce every year.

From May through October, a farmers' market is held at the Sunset Park location on Sundays. Several stories aboveground, under a vast open sky, neat rows of vegetables—heirloom tomatoes, eggplants, peppers, tomatillos, kale, chard, and an abundance of leafy greens—are set against intoxicating views of Manhattan across the East River. Birds, bees, and butterflies flutter among the meadow plantings of daisies, asters, and purple coneflowers. Giant sunflowers seem to dwarf the Empire State Building in the background. New York City seen from the farms is a greener and healthier city, alive with possibilities.

With a population close to nine million people, the city will always have to rely on food produced outside its limits, but rooftop farms like Brooklyn Grange do much more than provide New Yorkers with locally grown produce. "What we've created is not just a farm but a community hub, an education incubator for agriculture, and an urban park," said Flanner. Brooklyn Grange also founded a nonprofit, City Growers, which offers growing workshops for the city's public school students, connecting young people with nature and inspiring a new generation of urban farmers. During the worst months of the pandemic in 2020, the farm worked with Blundstone, the footwear company, to provide ten thousand pounds of produce to community-based organizations around the city.

Vegetables are not the only things thriving on Brooklyn Grange's farms in the sky. With their wide variety of organically grown plants and flowers, the farms' beehives reportedly fare better than those in rural farmland where monocrops and pesticides rule. Crop rotation, compost, and

established 2010   **total acreage** 5.6   **website** brooklyngrangefarm.com

cover crops—clover, oats, and vetch—ensure a healthy ecosystem. The farms bring many fringe benefits to the city: they divert millions of gallons of stormwater a year from the city's overtaxed sewer system, combat the heat island effect, clean the air, and reduce energy use for heating and cooling in the buildings underneath them. As cofounder Anastasia Cole Plakias observed, "While rooftop farms can never produce enough crops to feed our growing population, they have the power to stoke our appetite for what cities of the future should look like, serving up critical green infrastructure while connecting urbanites with our food systems, agriculture, and nature." Visit the farmers' market in Sunset Park, take a tour, or attend a workshop at the Navy Yard farm and catch a glimpse of the future of urban agriculture, pointing to a greener and more resilient city.

ABOVE: The wildflower plantings at the Sunset Park farm attract a host of insects, such as the black swallowtail butterfly, *right*. OPPOSITE: The farm in the sky, with a view of Manhattan.

The farm at the Navy Yard

The Secret Garden

A neighborhood legacy from two pioneers in Cobble Hill

All gardens have a story to tell. The Secret Garden, the only undeveloped piece of private land amid the brownstones in Cobble Hill, tells the unlikely story of two men, from different continents and races, who came to the neighborhood in the 1960s and built their life together.

Nathaniel LaMar was one of two Black students in Harvard's class of 1955, graduating Phi Beta Kappa with an award to study literature at Cambridge. His story "Creole Love Song" won first prize in a writing competition at Harvard and was included in *The Best American Short Stories* anthology of 1956. Christopher Adlington came to New York from England, intending to stay for a short term, but he never left. He trained as an accountant, but gardening was his passion.

For fifty years, Christopher cultivated a garden on a lot behind his and Nat's house in what was then a traditional Italian neighborhood. Working alone, he turned what had been a junkyard into a miniature English garden. Lilacs bloomed in spring, roses tumbled along the walls, and boxwood shrubs grew into giant balls. Catching glimpses of the garden through the chain-link fence, neighbors began calling it the Secret Garden, after Frances Hodgson Burnett's much-loved novel.

When Christopher died in 2015 and Nat became bedridden, Julia Lichtblau, who lives next door, took on the task of tending the garden. "I couldn't stand to let all of Christopher's work go to waste," she explained. Other neighbors began pitching in, with both time and money, to carry on Christopher's lifework. Before he passed away in 2022, Nat kept a watchful but approving eye as the new gardeners pruned the trees, mowed the lawn, sought treatment for a euonymus shrub afflicted with mildew, laid new paths, and added new plantings.

Taking up the entire lot of a typical row house, the garden is anchored by a majestic oak tree thought to be over two centuries old, dating back to the days when this part of Brooklyn was farmland. Just beyond the gate lies an open sunny lawn with borders that are in bloom from early spring until fall. A narrow stone path leads to the second part of the garden, where a weeping cherry tree shades primroses and pansies at its feet. Another small square lawn with an apricot tree ends at a retaining wall that drops down to the sunken shade garden.

The Secret Garden is no longer so secret. The doors are flung open to the public on Sunday mornings. Concerts and parties are held to celebrate the summer solstice, Halloween, and other holidays of the year. This slice of green space has become a hub for the neighborhood, where families put down their roots and children learn to garden.

In an essay published in *The Common*, Julia reflected on the value of the Secret Garden: "Christopher and Nat. Two men, one white, one Black. Pioneers in their era. They put down roots in Brooklyn and planted a garden. The garden takes no political stance. At the same time, one would have to be completely oblivious not to feel a resonance of that story in their garden. In a city obsessed with real estate, how about an alternate metric to value this particular plot of land? Say a hundred people a day pause to look through the chain-link, that's 36,500 moments a year. Over the last fifty years, that comes to 1,825,000 moments of peace, mystery, pleasure, surprise. How much is that worth?"

established 2015 **total acreage** 0.6 **entrance** 251 Degraw Street **public transit** Bergen St **F** **G**
website secretgardenbk.com

Naval Cemetery Landscape

A magical wildflower meadow and monarch way station under the shadow of the BQE

"A little magic in the heart of Brooklyn." "A quiet centering breath among the rest of the city." "A perfect place for handholds and soft feet and bumblebees." These are just some descriptions by visitors of the Naval Cemetery Landscape, the first open green space on the twenty-six-mile Brooklyn Waterfront Greenway.

With just 1.7 acres situated under the shadow of the bustling Brooklyn-Queens Expressway (BQE) on the southern edge of Williamsburg, the landscape is a small pocket of tranquility with an outsize impact and transformative power. This forgotten corner was reimagined as a park with a mission to heal both people and the land. For Milton Puryear, whose tenacity brought the project to fruition, it is a place for people, especially residents of the area long deprived of green spaces, to "immerse themselves in natural surroundings that provide relief from stress and help restore focus, attention, and personal resiliency."

It's also a place with a long and varied history. This slice of Williamsburg was part of Wallabout Bay, which got its name from the French-speaking Walloons from Holland who settled in the area in the early 1630s. For two centuries, they farmed the land, turning wet meadows into vegetable gardens and fruit orchards. After the Revolutionary War, the farms gave way to the navy shipbuilding facility. The Brooklyn Naval Hospital was built in the nineteenth century on one of the last farms to be sold. From 1831 to 1910, as many as two thousand sailors and marines (and their relatives) were laid to rest in the hospital's cemetery. In 1926, a little less than half of the remains were relocated to Cypress Hills National Cemetery, leaving hundreds

likely still buried on the site. For a few years it served as a ball field, and then it stood abandoned and fenced off for nearly a century until the Naval Cemetery Landscape opened in May 2016.

Entering through a pavilion on Williamsburg Street, visitors are greeted by a memorial meadow of tall native grasses sprinkled with purple coneflowers, blazing stars, brown-eyed Susans, wild bergamots, woodland sunflowers, and mountain mint. A sinuous black locust boardwalk—specially built to minimize disturbance to the hallowed ground—winds through the meadow like a floating river, conjuring up the wetland that once existed on-site. A grove of black cherry trees recalls the old orchards. An intersecting axis of granite blocks pays homage to the industrial past of the navy yard while also commemorating those buried in the site.

Once a place of death, the landscape is now humming with life. People gather to practice yoga among the wildflowers. Schoolchildren come to study the natural environment. Art shows and beekeeping and ecology classes are held throughout the year. The park is a refuge not only for humans but also for all creatures. Birds, butterflies, bees, moths, and all manner of insects thrive in abundance here.

The landscape is one of two Nature Sacred sites in New York City—the other being the Beach Forty-First Street Gardens in the Rockaways. As part of the organization's research on nature's effects on stressed communities, Nature Sacred installs in each of its sites a bench with a weatherproof box containing a journal for visitors to record their thoughts and reflections in. At the Naval Cemetery

established 2016   **total acreage** 1.7   **entrance** 63 Williamsburg Street West   **public transit** Flushing Av/Steuben St **B57** and Flushing Av/Kent Av **B48** buses; Brooklyn Navy Yard ferry stop **AST** **website** brooklyngreenway.org/naval-cemetery-landscape

Landscape, some park goers fill the journals with drawings. Others pen lines of poetry. More than a few unburden their deepest troubles. One visitor happily logged ten sightings of the golden northern bumblebee, a listed vulnerable species, within thirty minutes in the meadow. Messages of gratitude abound.

The journal entries attest to the magic that engulfs you as soon as you enter the Naval Cemetery Landscape. The roar of traffic fades into the background. You slacken your pace. You hear the birds. You see the insects. You pay attention to the green life that's all around you, learning the names of the park's flora and fauna, perhaps for the first time. The world reveals itself in a whole new language. Spend some time in this place and it might change your way of thinking.

PREVIOUS PAGES: The meadow in summer. ABOVE, *left*: Granite blocks commemorate those buried on the site; *right*: Purple coneflowers. OPPOSITE: Woodland sunflowers and blue asters.

Shirley Chisholm State Park

Scenic trails and wildflower meadows on the shores of Jamaica Bay

At Brooklyn's newest green space, Shirley Chisholm State Park, visitors have myriad ways to engage with nature. Rising 130 feet above sea level, the park offers ten miles of hiking and biking trails through spectacular prairie grasslands and wildflower meadows on gently sloping hills with views over Jamaica Bay. Three miles of shoreline and three tidal creeks with picnic areas, a fishing pier, and kayak launches afford ample recreational activities. "Bike libraries," run by Bike New York at the Pennsylvania and Fountain Entrances, provide free bike rentals in warmer months. An environmental education center cultivates naturalists of all ages with free programs throughout the year. Park rangers lead night hikes to study the stars and daytime guided bird walks. With its diverse ecological habitats, the park has attracted over 150 species of birds, from songbirds to raptors, as well as many wading and shorebird species. Short-eared owls have been spotted spreading their wings over the grasslands, as have spring visitors like warblers, tanagers, orioles, and grosbeaks. Northern harriers hunt upon these hills while great blue herons wait patiently on the shore of Hendrix Creek for their meals. It is no wonder that the park is part of the New York State Birding Trail, which includes thirty-three bird-watching stations around the five boroughs.

To visitors who now enjoy the waterfront park, it is unimaginable that these 407 acres of native grasslands, wildflower meadows, and fishing pier were once deemed a "significant threat to the public health or environment." Decades ago, the city had plans to make a park and wildlife preserve on the northern shore of Jamaica Bay, including the land on which Shirley Chisholm State Park now sits. The project was favored by New York parks commissioner Robert Moses, and a parcel of 885 acres of land originally purchased by the city for development was transferred to the Parks Department, much of it marshlands to be filled in to create access to the water for fishing, boating, and swimming.

Moses's vision never materialized. By 1974, part of the area was developed into one of the largest housing complexes in the city, and expanses of filled-in marshlands on Pennsylvania and Fountain Avenues were being used as landfills. Garbage would eventually cover more than 407 acres, reaching over 130 feet high, full of toxins like DDT and asbestos, as well as illegally dumped chemical waste. Even after the closure of the landfills in 1985, "runoff containing heavy metals, oil, pesticides and PCBs flowed into Jamaica Bay," according to the *New York Times*. Health concerns led to the long and challenging effort instigated by local residents to rehabilitate the toxic site.

The creation of Shirley Chisholm State Park began with a project that capped the two landfills with a layer of plastic and three feet of clean soil—1.2 million cubic feet worth, "enough to fill nearly 100,000 dump trucks," according to the park's website. In 2004, the first seeds were sown on the Pennsylvania Avenue Landfill. Shrubs and trees were planted a year later. Within a couple of years, thirty-five thousand trees and shrubs and native grassland species had been planted at the two sites to create a diverse ecosystem of coastal meadows, wetlands, and woodlands.

established 2019   total acreage 407   entrances 1750 Pennsylvania Avenue and 950 Fountain Avenue   public transit Seaview Av/Pennsylvania Av **B82**, **B83**, **BM2**, and **BM5** buses   website parks.ny.gov/parks/shirleychisholm

The park debuted in 2019 with the Pennsylvania Avenue section, followed by the Fountain Avenue section in 2021. It was named for the trailblazing educator and child welfare activist Shirley Chisholm, who became the first Black US congresswoman in 1968. Her spirit looms large at the park's Pennsylvania Entrance in a mural by the Brooklyn artist Danielle Mastrion.

Throughout her political career, Chisholm fought to improve the health and wellness of underserved communities. The dedication of the community in this corner of Brooklyn brought her namesake park to life to improve the health and wellness of not just local residents but also the environment and the wildlife that now thrive on what were once toxic landfills.

ABOVE: The park offers ten miles of hiking and biking trails over meadows and woodlands brimming with wildlife.
OPPOSITE: A mural of Congresswoman Shirley Chisholm at the entrance to the park.

Queens

Jamaica Bay Wildlife Refuge

A bird sanctuary poised against the Manhattan skyline

Jamaica Bay Wildlife Refuge is a rare gem, a wilderness on the edge of the nation's busiest city. Occupying more than half of the open waters and wetlands of Jamaica Bay, this green space is one of the last wild places in the five boroughs and earned a spot on the list of the top one hundred places for birding in the world.

Poised at the southernmost meeting point of Queens and Brooklyn, Jamaica Bay's twelve thousand acres of water, marsh, meadowland, beaches, dunes, and forest are the city's greatest ecological treasures. A thriving shellfish industry once flourished in the bay, before overdevelopment and industrialization slowly began to destroy it. By the 1920s, increasing pollution in the bay's water led to a ban on shellfishing. In 1938, the parks commissioner, Robert Moses, lamented, "Jamaica Bay faces the blight of bad planning, polluted water, and garbage dumping." Fifteen years later, the city established Jamaica Bay Wildlife Refuge, making it a sanctuary for both New Yorkers and wildlife. To attract migratory birds, Moses commissioned the creation of two large freshwater ponds that remain the dominant features of the park today. Herbert Johnson, the first superintendent of the refuge, initiated a massive planting—berry shrubs, beach grass, wild roses, and other flora—to restore miles of deteriorated marshland. The efforts paid off, as a news story in the *New York Times* two years later reported the return of snowy egrets and black crown herons, as well as an increase in striped bass and flounder in the bay.

But pollution continued to plague Jamaica Bay. Excessive nitrogen in the water stemming from four city sewage treatment plants caused harmful algae blooms that choked all marine life, which in turn affected local and migrating birds that fed on it. In just over seven decades in the last century, the salt marshes in the bay shrank by more than half. In 1972, Jamaica Bay became part of the Gateway National Recreation Area, which includes the People's Beach at Jacob Riis Park and Sandy Hook in New Jersey, all managed by the National Park Service.

Decades of cleanup and efforts to slow the erosion of the bay's marsh islands, advocated by environmental and community groups, have improved the health of the bay. Today its natural and man-made habitats—salt marsh, fresh and brackish water ponds, intertidal marshes, meadows, and woods—host wildlife as diverse as the human population of New York City. As a critical stopover area along the Eastern Flyway migration route, Jamaica Bay is one of the best bird-watching locations in the western hemisphere. More than 330 species of birds—nearly half of all the species in the Northeast—and over 60 species of butterflies have been spotted here. Ospreys, nearly decimated in the 1950s and '60s by the use of DDT, have made a hearty comeback at the refuge, taking up residence on the park's fifteen man-made nesting platforms when they return from their winter vacation in Central and South America. In spring, the bird population swells with warblers, tree swallows, and red-winged blackbirds making their nests along the trail surrounding the West Pond. The berry-laden branches of eastern red cedars are the province of waxwings and kinglets, while the marshes and ponds draw a great number of colorful heron species: green, little blue, and yellow-crowned night heron, to name just a few.

established 1972   total acreage 12,600   entrance 175-10 Cross Bay Boulevard   public transit Broad Channel Ⓐ Ⓢ   website nps.gov/gate/learn/historyculture/jamaica-bay-wildlife-refuge.htm

The refuge also affords the best chance in New York City to spot the rare tricolored heron. At the annual Raptorama Festival, which celebrates the fall migration of birds of prey through the greater New York City area, children of all ages are introduced to live close-up views of hawks, owls, and eagles while others enjoy a guided bird walk to see the many hawk species on their flight south for the winter.

The bay's marsh fringes are also home to eighty species of fish, as well as other marine life, including one of the largest populations of horseshoe crabs. Other permanent and visiting residents include endangered and threatened species like peregrine falcons, piping plovers, and the Atlantic Ridley sea turtle.

Jamaica Bay continues to evolve, shaped by natural forces that form a constant pattern

PREVIOUS PAGES: A red-winged blackbird resting on a tree in the marsh around the West Pond in winter.
ABOVE AND OPPOSITE, *from left to right*: The West Pond in winter; as tree cavities become rarer in

of sedimentation and erosion. The damaging human impacts on its ecosystem over the past couple of centuries have been reversed only through the passionate commitment of people for whom this wild place is a beloved resource. Hike along the trails of the wildlife refuge on a summer day and experience the vast expanse of the marshes and the water. Smell the salty air. Listen to the calls of songbirds. Look for ruby-throated hummingbirds, cedar waxwings, and American redstarts in the meadows. See the flocks of floating ducks and foraging wading birds against the backdrop of the Manhattan skyline and the jet planes taking off and landing at JFK Airport. At Jamaica Bay Wildlife Refuge, the fragile connection between the natural and urban worlds of New York City is rendered vividly and beautifully.

New York City, tree swallows have turned to the many bird boxes around the refuge for nesting; West Pond is an important wintering area for waterfowl; a yellow-rumped warbler in the woodland.

Fort Tilden

A pristine ocean beach for watching migrating hawks

Few New Yorkers are aware that there are more than 14 miles of public beaches on the city's 520-mile coastline. The image of a New York City beach in the popular imagination is either Coney Island, with sunbathers packed like sardines in a can, or Rockaway Beach, which has become a vibrant surf scene in recent years, with an exciting food culture that attracts New Yorkers from all boroughs. Southwest of Rockaway Beach is the equally popular People's Beach at Jacob Riis Park. Farther south, away from the crowd, toward the end of Rockaway Peninsula, before Breezy Point at the tip, lies Fort Tilden, with miles of the most pristine ocean beaches in the city.

First established in 1917, Fort Tilden served as part of the harbor defenses of New York. During the height of the Cold War, it was the launch site of the Nike Hercules missile system for the US medium and high-altitude long-range air defense. The army base was decommissioned in 1974, and ownership of the site was transferred to the National Park Service, making it part of the Gateway National Recreation Area.

In the half century since then, Fort Tilden has been reclaimed by nature, making it one of the most compelling landscapes in New York City. Abandoned bunkers and missile sites wrapped in twisting vines serve as an urban canvas for graffiti artists. Derelict batteries are swallowed up by dense vegetation or almost entirely buried under the dunes, melding into the natural maritime woodland that has sprung up over the decades and now makes up a large part of the 309-acre park. A nature trail from the beach to one of the batteries, laid out in the late 1970s, is now overgrown, in parts overtaken by poison ivy, which makes exploring the paths a real adventure. Alternatively, a wide cement road between the beach and coastal forest is great for biking.

Limited parking has kept Fort Tilden's beach relatively quiet. The more intrepid beachgoers who venture the ten-minute walk from the promenade at Jacob Riis will find beyond the grassy dunes a serene beach with pristine white sand. Even on a hot summer day, sunbathers are few and far between, sharing the peaceful coastline with hikers, fishers angling for bluefish and fluke, and birders—in fall, Fort Tilden is the best place to watch for hawks on their southward migration.

The park is also home to the endangered piping plovers, which fly from the Gulf of Mexico and the Caribbean to New York for nesting season. The tiny sand-colored birds make their home on these shores from mid-March until August. They lay eggs in shallow scrapes in the sand, making them vulnerable to human disturbance. Both the NYC Parks Department and National Park Service monitor the population of this threatened shorebird, closing off parts of the beach every year to protect plovers looking for a safe place to start a family.

The Indigenous Canarsee people who inhabited Long Island called these barrier beaches between Jamaica Bay and the Atlantic Ocean Reckowacky, meaning "neck of land," "lonely place," or "place of waters bright." At the top of Battery Harris East, accessible by wooden stairs, the sweeping view at sunset—the painted sky above the sparkling sea—reaffirms the spirit of this place evoked in its original name.

established 1974   **total acreage** 309   **entrance** Rockaway Point Boulevard, Breezy Point
public transit Rockaway Park–Beach 116 St **A** **S**; Rockaway ferry stop **RW**
website nps.gov/gate/learn/historyculture/fort-tilden.htm

Isamu Noguchi Foundation and Garden Museum

A sanctuary of earth, water, stone, and trees

In 1961, the sculptor Isamu Noguchi moved out of his studio in Greenwich Village to a remote corner in Long Island City, where he turned a one-story factory into a home and studio. Less than a decade later, needing more space, he purchased a 1920s redbrick building across the street. Once occupied by a photo-engraving plant, the 31,000-square-foot, two-story building came with a large courtyard. Next he bought the gas station next door, which he razed, constructing a concrete building in its place. Occupying the entire triangular city block, these two properties today make up the footprint of the Isamu Noguchi Foundation and Garden Museum.

This New York gem opened in 1985, three years before the artist passed away. A path from the concrete entry pavilion leads to an outdoor garden of stone sculptures arranged on gravel ground among the trees. Ivy-covered walls enclose the garden under an open sky. For the artist, the museum's garden was "a metaphor for the world," meaning a space where one could think about one's place in nature.

Born to an American writer and a Japanese poet, Noguchi spent most of his childhood in Japan. He entered Columbia University as a premed student, only to drop out to become an artist. He returned to Japan to work with clay and study gardens after a stint as an assistant for Romanian sculptor Constantin Brâncuși and eight months in Beijing studying calligraphy and brush drawing. Although Noguchi created sculpture gardens from Jerusalem and Paris to Los Angeles and Sapporo, the garden in New York is his most personal and intimate. The works on display, which he describes as stone sculptures

whose "weathering seems to coincide . . . with our own sense of historical time," were assembled here by the artist himself. Noguchi selected the trees and plants, all native to Japan, the United States, or both, paying particular attention to their texture and form. Birch, pines, azaleas, bamboo, weeping cherry, magnolia, and mounds of juniper create an environment that changes with the seasons, reflecting the passage of time.

At less than two-thirds of an acre, the garden is modest in scale yet expansive in scope. "If sculpture is the rock," Noguchi once wrote, "it is also the space between rocks and between the rock and a man, and the communication and contemplation between." The garden is a work of art to be experienced through all its elements—stone, water, trees, but also light, weather—inviting reflections on beauty as shaped by nature and time. The stone sculptures are slowly being worn as the trees continue to grow through the years. The katsura tree, planted as a sapling, now spreads its canopy over nearly the entire garden.

Noguchi called his garden museum "an oasis on the edge of a black hole." At the heart of the garden is *The Well* (*Variation on a Tsukubai*), Noguchi's take on the traditional Japanese washbasin provided at the entrance to a holy place. Water flows, silently but unceasingly, from the top of a stone column, forming circles that ripple outward until they spill over and dissolve down the sides—a poetic meditation on the perpetual passage of time and the constant renewal of nature. It's well worth the pilgrimage to this corner of Long Island City to experience Noguchi's legacy and his gift to the people of New York.

established 1985   total acreage 0.62   entrance 9-01 33rd Road at Vernon Boulevard
public transit Vernon Blvd/33 Rd **Q103** bus; Astoria ferry stop **AST**   website noguchi.org

Gantry Plaza State Park

A riverside pleasure ground with spectacular views of Midtown Manhattan

The waterfront in Long Island City once teemed with barges, tugboats, and railcars that transported goods from the factories in Queens to Manhattan across the East River. Gantry Plaza State Park, known locally as simply Gantry Park, celebrates this industrial history with the icons of its past, the monumental gantries—floating bridges once used to transfer freight cars to river barges. With striking panoramic views of the Manhattan skyline, plentiful recreational facilities, as well as contemplative areas—all built on former industrial edifices—the park jump-started the transformation of New York's postindustrial shorelines into vibrant green spaces.

Encompassing a former dock facility and part of a former PepsiCo bottling plant, this twelve-acre park makes the most of its natural shoreline along the East River. Four piers, each different in size, shape, and use, project into the river like water follies. The Fishing Pier, on the southern end of the park, is equipped with a free-form stainless steel fish-cleaning station, complete with a sink and a disposal area. The Stargazing Pier, screened from the shore lights, has curvaceous wooden chaises, all the better to look up to the sky.

The large plaza, with the skyline framed by the gantries, accommodates thirty thousand spectators for the Fourth of July fireworks or a summer concert. Kids can cool off in the mist fountain on scorching summer days and play on the colorful art deco playground. Along the shore at the southern end, blocks of granite are clustered among tall grass and shrubbery as if they had always been there. Rail lines cut through the planted beds to reveal another layer of history in this place.

A stroll along the promenade gives visitors a chance to take in the scenic view of the East River, with the Manhattan skyline as its backdrop. Along the way, luxuriant lawns and promontories shaded by willow trees, Adirondack chairs painted bright red nestled in flower beds, and wooden benches facing the river provide places to rest or congregate. At the northern end stands the iconic Pepsi-Cola sign from 1936, another vestige of Gantry Park's former existence.

When the park first opened in 1998, the *New York Times* architecture critic Herbert Muschamp praised, among other things, its "intimate immensity," declaring the gantries "as powerful as the triumphal arches and classical monuments built by the City Beautiful Movement a century ago." Gantry Park marked a seminal moment in New York City's rediscovery of its waterfronts: the site's rugged beauty and industrial archaeology gave the city's future parks a new visual language (as seen in the preservation of the railroad tracks in the planting beds on the High Line; see page 123).

With the hulking blackened iron gantries as its talisman, this riverside pleasure ground bridges its history to its future as it celebrates the waterfront, giving New Yorkers new ways to experience one of the city's greatest natural assets. From thriving industry to derelict wasteland, this stretch of the Queens shoreline is now home to not just one but two of New York's most spectacular and ecological parks, Gantry Plaza State Park and its neighbor, Hunter's Point South Park (see page 239).

established 1998   total acreage 12   entrance 4-09 47th Road   public transit Hunters Point South ferry stop **ER** and Long Island City ferry stop **AST**; Vernon Blvd/Jackson Av **7** and 21st St/Jackson Av **G**; Long Island City LIRR **Oyster Bay** and **Port Jefferson** lines
website parks.ny.gov/parks/gantryplaza

Smiling Hogshead Ranch

An offbeat farm in a former rail yard

Not too distant from Brooklyn Grange's Long Island City rooftop farm (see page 201), down on earth, Smiling Hogshead Ranch is a charmingly ramshackle urban farm with a big mission: to create a culture that empowers and connects communities through ecology, education, and collaboration.

"We were created in 2011 as a guerrilla garden," explained environmental educator and Smiling Hogshead Ranch founder Gil Lopez, "which means that we didn't have permission to come onto the land, clean up the trash that was here, clear out the weeds and the rocks, and cultivate the soil." The land was once part of Degnon Terminal, a large freight rail yard serving Long Island City's industries. Ownership of the terminal was transferred to Long Island Railroad in 1928, but the terminal was disconnected from the rest of the rail network in 1989.

It took a year and a half for the property's current owner, the Metropolitan Transit Authority, to find out about the garden being made on the abandoned railroad track. Luckily, they extended a garden license agreement to the group, officially founding Smiling Hogshead Ranch. (Its unusual name was inspired by the pig skeleton uncovered on the site by the gardeners.) Surrounded by sprawling industrial warehouses, the farm is a small slice of green haven with a cornucopia of herbs, flowers, fruit, and vegetables, all organically grown.

On sunny days, eastern tiger swallowtail butterflies can be spotted feeding on milkweed while their black swallowtail cousins feast on catmint. In late summer, cucumbers and kabocha squashes hang in abundance from trellises. The raised beds are smothered in kale, chard, and herbs. Tall and fragrant fennels, marigolds, and cosmos spill over the paths. Clusters of grapes hang from the vine, ripening from the warmth of the sun. Dark juicy blackberries grow from prickly brambles. At the western end of the farm, a path along the old track is left overgrown with oddly shaped gourds. Brightly painted picnic tables and colorful artwork lend a cheerful atmosphere.

Both wild and bountiful, the ranch is a rare place in this industrial corner of the city where gardeners young and old can enjoy being out in the sun, getting their hands dirty, and growing their own food. It's also become more than just a farm. Smiling Hogshead Ranch touts itself as a community garden by day and a social club and cultural venue by night. The annual International Sunflower Guerrilla Gardening Day in May brings together volunteers to share seeds and sow sunflowers all over the city. A composting program and a range of workshops—from wreath making to biodynamic composting to chess lessons—as well as concerts, plays, and food festivals keep the farm connected with the local community. An extensive outreach program has the farm working with school groups and organizations helping formerly incarcerated people.

Come and partake in the community spirit of Smiling Hogshead Ranch. During the growing season, the garden hosts "Farming Fridays," when members and volunteers gather to complete garden chores in the afternoon and sit down for a potluck dinner at 7:00 p.m. All are welcome, and depending on the mood, a Hula-Hoop dance party may close the evening.

established 2011 **total acreage** 0.5 **entrance** 25-30 Skillman Avenue
public transit Hunters Point Av ❼; Hunterspoint Avenue LIRR **Montauk**, **Oyster Bay**, and **Port Jefferson** lines **website** smilinghogsheadranch.org

Hunter's Point South Park

A blueprint for future waterfront parks

Seamlessly adjoining Gantry Plaza State Park (see page 233) as part of the thirty-acre waterfront redevelopment is Hunter's Point South Park, New York's model of resiliency against the inexorable flooding patterns and rising sea level. Flanked by Newtown Creek and the East River, this glorious park combines a vision of nature that harks back to the island's precolonial days with a twenty-first-century approach to green infrastructure.

Once home to heavy industry, Hunter's Point South Park today is a bustling focal point for the expanding local community. It has also attracted New Yorkers from other boroughs, especially Brooklynites who live a short bike ride away. For Manhattanites, the park is a five-minute ferry ride from Midtown. On any given day, the place is lively with bikers, joggers, and people strolling through the grasslands and flowers. Yoga practitioners hold their poses against the rising sun. Volleyball matches play out on the sandy beach. Kayakers navigate the waters of Newtown Creek. Children fill the playground. At the end of the day, young and old gather on the pier to watch the fiery sun dip behind the Empire State Building.

Designed by the landscape architect Thomas Balsley of SWA/Balsley, in collaboration with the architects at Weiss/Manfredi and the engineering firm Arup, Hunter's Point South Park has two distinct sections. The first and northern part of the park, mostly for active recreational use, was completed in 2013. Railroad tracks were transformed into flower beds. The dog run pays homage to its former iteration as a lumberyard with stacked-wood benches. The main sunken oval lawn, half covered in artificial turf, is used as an athletic field and concert stage, with its curving steps as seating—but it doubles as a retaining basin for floodwaters. When Superstorm Sandy swept through the park before its completion, floodwater was held in the lawn and receded with the tide, leaving the site undamaged. Bioswale—a system of stormwater management using deep-rooted plants—also lines the street on the edge of the park, collecting and filtering stormwater with flowering gardens that double as wildlife habitats.

The second section of the park, opened in 2018, offers a wilder and more contemplative landscape. Intimate seating niches nestled in birch groves line the path along the riverbank. A promontory carved out of the former forty-foot-high landfill commands an expansive vista along the riverbend at the park's southernmost end. The designers reinvented the water's edge with tidal marshes and built a cantilevered overlook suspended twenty feet above the wetlands, where native grasses were planted in what is known as a soft approach to flood control. Unlike hard infrastructure like a seawall, the wetlands allow the park to "bend and not break," in Balsley's words, during a superstorm by absorbing and releasing stormwater gently.

Forgoing irrigation, the designers chose a palette of native salt-tolerant plants and trees to create a diverse and enduring landscape that also sustains wildlife. These include native coastal grasses, goldenrod, joe-pye weed, purple coneflower, beach plum, serviceberry, honey locust, black gum, pitch pine, and willow oak. On the grassy promontory, a thick carpet of daffodils in early April announces the coming of warmer months with irresistible cheer.

established 2013   total acreage 10   entrance Center Boulevard between 50th Avenue and 2nd Street   public transit Hunters Point South ferry stop **ER**; Vernon Blvd–Jackson Av **7** and 21st St **G**; Long Island City LIRR **Oyster Bay** and **Port Jefferson** lines   website hunterspointparks.org

The East River is really a tidal strait, and before the arrival of European settlers, this shoreline was a series of salt marshes. By the twentieth century, industry had obliterated the area's rich ecology. Landfill from the excavation of the Midtown Tunnel reconfigured its topography, leaving an irregular water's edge, unsightly mounds of debris, and decaying piers. The landfill mound north of the overlook was resculpted

into a small island, separated by a tidal marsh and embraced by a grove of black gum trees. A curving footbridge over the marsh leads to a circular lawn with an installation by the artist Nobuho Nagasawa. Seven luminescent sculptures depicting the phases of the moon celebrate the tidal forces that shape this shoreline.

The new wetlands are protected from the erosive power of the East River's strong tidal

ABOVE AND OPPOSITE, *from left to right*: A tidal marsh turns a former landfill into an island; the second section of the park offers an urban wildness; the zigzagging trail brings visitors to the water's edge; a cantilevered overlook

currents by a riprap—a permanent ground cover of loose stones—embankment, planted with both grasses and clusters of trees. The undulating waves of grasses, backlit by the light bouncing off the river, have an ineffable wild beauty. Juxtaposed against the Manhattan skyline, they evoke the city's past and intimate its future.

The center of gravity in the expansive southern section of the park is the overlook that floats twenty feet above the tidal marsh to frame the spectacle of the skyline. From this dramatic focal point, several paths unfurl like tendrils, bringing park goers directly into the wetlands or giving them a perch to view the landscape from above, shifting perspectives and alternating the focus from the river to Manhattan's skyscrapers. A trail descends to the water's edge, zigzagging along the way to encourage a slower

hovers above the tidal marsh, offering vistas of the East River and the Manhattan skyline. FOLLOWING PAGES: Daffodils and other spring flowers on the promontory lawn.

pace and offer a succession of orientations. Twice a day, the East River floods the wetlands and recedes with the tides, blurring the edges between land and water. The trail takes visitors into this liminal space, while kayaks allow them to access the river directly. This intimate and lyrical connection with the tidal shoreline, against the immensity of the urban landscape, immeasurably expands New Yorkers' experience of the city itself.

The dialogue between the urban and the pastoral is at the heart of the park's evocative beauty. The essence of New York City is distilled in Hunter's Point South Park's landscape of marsh, river, and cityscape, echoing Walt Whitman's ecstatic musing in "Mannahatta" nearly two centuries ago: "The beautiful city, the city of hurried and sparkling waters! The city of spires and masts! The city nested in bays! My city!"

ABOVE: Terraces and benches along the trail offer places to pause for reflection at the water's edge. OPPOSITE: The marsh trail takes visitors into the liminal space between land and water.

Acknowledgments

It has been an immense joy to research, write, and photograph this book. I owe an enormous debt to Eric W. Sanderson and his revelatory book *Mannahatta*, which renders the ecological history of Manhattan vividly, both in words and images. I am grateful to all the landscape architects, gardeners, park workers, and community organizers who have created and maintained the rich tapestry of green spaces in New York City. Thank you to everyone who generously gave their time to talk to me about their work. To Warrie Price for her tireless efforts on behalf of the Battery. To Rebecca McMackin for her advocacy of ecological horticulture. To Bella Ciabattoni and all the gardeners at Brooklyn Bridge Park. To Jason Siebenmorgen at Michael Van Valkenburgh Associates for his work on Brooklyn Bridge Park. To Jeffrey Longhenry for his work on the Naval Cemetery Landscape. To Donald Loggins, the one remaining founding member of the Liz Christy Community Garden, whose stories of the garden's early days are a treasure. To Sarah Burd-Sharps and Greg O'Connell at Pier 44 Waterfront Garden for nurturing the community spirit of Red Hook. To Thomas Balsley at SWA/Balsley and the architects at Weiss/Manfredi for their beautiful work on Hunter's Point South Park. To Julia Lichtblau at the Secret Garden for sharing her moving essay on the value of this small plot of green. To Carly Still and Yvette Weaver for their ministrations to the beautiful gardens at the Met Cloisters. To Anastasia Cole Plakias at Brooklyn Grange for taking urban farming into the future. To Brian Sullivan and Todd Forrest at the New York Botanical Garden for their stewardship of one of New York's greatest natural assets.

I am thankful to everyone who facilitated access to the parks and gardens for photography: Elizabeth Reina-Longoria at the Brooklyn Botanic Garden, Victoria Yan at Brooklyn Grange, Elizabeth Butson and Susan Sipos at Jefferson Market Garden, Jeffrey Kindley at the Lotus Garden, Anna Bakis and Remy Schwartz at the Naval Cemetery Landscape, Ariel Handelman at the New York Botanical Garden, and Judith Robinson at the West Side Community Garden.

The green spaces of New York City would not be the same without the support of a multitude of organizations, and I am especially appreciative of the following: the Battery Conservancy, the Brooklyn Bridge Park Conservancy, the Brooklyn Greenway Initiative, the Central Park Conservancy, the City Parks Foundation, Friends of Pelham Bay Park and the hundreds of neighborhood Friends of Parks groups throughout the city, the Green Guerillas, the Hunters Point Parks Conservancy, the Madison Square Park Conservancy, NYC Parks GreenThumb, the New York Restoration Project, the Prospect Park Alliance, and the Trust for Public Land.

It was a profound pleasure to work with Vanessa Holden, whose expert design and vision shaped this book beyond what I could imagine. I am very grateful for her friendship and support of my work. Warm thanks to Carla Glasser, who brought this project to me during the difficult months of the pandemic. I am thankful to the team at Artisan— including Bridget Monroe Itkin, Lia Ronnen, Suet Chong, Sibylle Kazeroid, Barbara Peragine, and Nancy Murray—for shepherding this project from beginning to end.

Lastly, deepest thanks to my husband, Julian Wass, and my daughter, Lily Wass, who have accompanied me in all of my life's greatest adventures.